OXFORDSHIRE

OXFORD, THE COTSWOLDS, & THE CHERWELL VALLEY

Nick Moon

This book is the first in a series of two providing a comprehensive coverage of walks throughout the whole of Oxfordshire (except the Chiltern part already covered in 'Chiltern Walks : Oxfordshire and West Buckinghamshire' by the same author). The walks included vary in length from 3.3 to 12.0 miles, but the majority are in, or have options in, the 5- to 7-miles range popular for half-day walks, although suggestions of possible combinations of walks are given for those preferring a full day's walk.

Each walk text gives details of nearby places of interest and is accompanied by a specially drawn map of the route which also indicates local pubs and a skeleton road network.

The author, Nick Moon, has lived on the Oxfordshire border or regularly visited the county all his life and has, for twenty-five years, been an active member of the Oxford Fieldpaths Society, which seeks to protect and improve the county's footpath and bridleway network. Thanks to the help and encouragement of the late Don Gresswell MBE, he was introduced to the writing books of walks and has since written or contributed to a number of publications in this field.

O·F·S

OTHER PUBLICATIONS BY NICK MOON:

Oxfordshire Walks:
Oxfordshire Walks 1: Oxford, the Cotswolds and the
Cherwell Valley new edition 1998
Oxfordshire Walks 2: Oxford, The Downs and The Thames Valley 1995

Chiltern Walks Trilogy:
Chiltern Walks 1: Hertfordshire, Bedfordshire and North
Buckinghamshire: Book Castle new edition 1996
Chiltern Walks 2: Buckinghamshire: Book Castle new edition 1997
Chiltern Walks 3: Oxfordshire and West Buckinghamshire:
Book Castle new edition 1996

Family Walks 1: Chilterns – South 1997
Family Walks 2: Chilterns – North 1998

Complete Books:
Walks for Motorists: Chilterns (Southern Area): Frederick Warne 1979
Walks for Motorists: Chilterns (Northern Area): Frederick Warne 1979
Walks in the Hertfordshire Chilterns : Shire 1986

Contributions:
Chiltern Society Footpath Maps: a number of walk descriptions –
also all map checking since c. 1975
Walks in the Countryside around London: W Foulsham & Co Ltd. 1985
Walker's Britain: Pan 1982
Walker's Britain II: Pan 1986

First published April 1994
New edition April 1998
By The Book Castle
12 Church Street, Dunstable, Bedfordshire

© Nick Moon, 1998

Computer Typeset by Keyword, Aldbury, Herts.
Printed in Great Britain by Antony Rowe Ltd., Chippenham, Wilts.

ISBN 1 871199 78 6

Cover photograph: Blenheim Palace and Grand Bridge (Walk 25).
© Nick Moon.

CONTENTS

Oxfordshire Walks : Oxford, The Cotswolds & The Cherwell Valley:
List of Walks

Possible Longer Walks Produced by Combining Walks Described in the Book

Walks						Miles	Km
2	+	3				13.5	21.7
2	+	3	+	4A		21.8	35.2
2	+	3	+	4(A–B)		18.9	30.4
3	+	4A				14.9	24.0
3	+	4(A–B)				11.9	19.2
7	+	9A				15.3	24.6
7	+	9B				11.2	18.0
10A	+	11A				16.6	26.8
10A	+	11A	+	12		22.4	36.1
10A	+	11C				12.8	20.6
10A	+	11C	+	12		18.6	30.0
10B	+	11A				14.5	23.4
10B	+	11A	+	12		20.4	32.8
10B	+	11C				10.7	17.2
10B	+	11C	+	12		16.5	26.6
11A	+	12				14.0	22.6
11C	+	12				10.2	16.5
13	+	18A				12.7	20.4
13	+	18A	+	19A		22.1	35.7
13	+	18A	+	19C		16.5	26.5
13	+	18B				10.9	17.6
13	+	18B	+	19A		20.4	32.8
13	+	18B	+	19C		14.7	23.6
15	+	16				15.0	24.2
18A	+	19A				15.0	24.2
18A	+	19C				9.3	15.0
18B	+	19A				13.2	21.3
18B	+	19C				7.5	12.1
23	+	29				19.4	31.3
24	+	25A				15.3	24.6
24	+	25B				13.1	21.1

N.B. The above combinations may vary in length depending on the starting point and linking routes used. The figures given here represent the shortest feasible routes using links indicated on the plans.

INTRODUCTION

This book is the first of two published by the Book Castle in association with the Oxford Fieldpaths Society describing walks throughout most of Oxfordshire, excluding only the Chiltern area already covered by 'Chiltern Walks : Oxfordshire and West Buckinghamshire' by the same author. Apart from the Downs and Chilterns in the south of the county, much of Oxfordshire remains to be discovered by all but local walkers, although it has a great variety of attractive landscapes to offer and many of its villages represent real gems of vernacular architecture. The resultant lack of use of the paths together with past neglect by landowners and local authorities led to many paths becoming obstructed and overgrown, but, in recent years, many have been restored to use and thanks to the kind co-operation of the County Council's Countryside Service and Bridges Department it is hoped that the more serious problems encountered in the preparation of this book will be resolved prior to publication.

This volume covers the northern half of Oxfordshire roughly north of a line from Burford through Witney and Oxford to Wheatley. While this area is one of great diversity, it is united by the fact that most of its villages are largely built of stone and much of the area witnessed confrontation during the Civil War when Charles I fled from London and set up his headquarters in Oxford.

Its southwestern segment is formed by the beautiful Cotswold river valleys of the Windrush, Evenlode, Glyme and Dorn separated by ridges much of which were once covered by the ancient Forest of Wychwood. Here the grey limestone of the Cotswolds predominates with slate roofs gradually giving way to thatch and dry-stone walls becoming fewer the further east one goes. While much of the land is now arable, the great historic parks such as Cornbury, Ditchley, Blenheim and Heythrop with their associated woodland ensure variety.

Further north the colour of the stone changes to the reddish hue of the ironstone Redlands and a high ridge marking the Warwickshire boundary separates the valleys of Cherwell tributaries from the Midland plain. Here the landscape is relatively bare with few trees; and a number of single hills and the fading scars of ironstone workings give it a strange appearance but with its sparse population and wide views, this remote corner of the county is well worth exploring.

To the east of the Cotswolds and Redlands is the Cherwell valley (pronounced 'Charwell' in Oxford but 'Cherwell' further north) which, together with the gap in the hills north of Banbury, has always formed a natural route to the Midlands. Despite the construction of the Oxford Canal, the Oxford–Birmingham railway line and more recently the M40, the valley has remained a place of great beauty to which the canal and some fine brick railway viaducts have actually contributed.

Further east, an attractive ridge separates the Cherwell valley from a wide flat plain drained by the River Ray, to the north of which is a pleasant low ridge with scattered woods, parkland and wide views into Buckinghamshire, forming the watershed between the Thames basin and the Great Ouse valley. Finally, to the southeast of the River Ray and Otmoor, a unique waterlogged fen, is a range of hills extending from Oxford northeastwards into Buckinghamshire with the scattered remains of the ancient forests of Shotover and Bernwood and superb views to the north and eastwards towards the Chilterns.

The majority of walks in this book are in, or have options in, the 5–7 miles range, which is justifiably popular for half-day walks, but, for the less energetic or for short winter afternoons, a few shorter versions are indicated in the text, while others can be devised with the help of a map. In addition, a number of walks in the 7–12 miles range are included for those preferring a leisurely day's walk or for longer spring and summer afternoons, while a list of possible combinations of walks is provided for those favouring a full day's walk of up to 22 miles.

Details of how to reach the starting points by car and where to park are given in the introductory information to each walk and any convenient railway stations are shown on the accompanying plan. As bus services are liable to frequent change, including information in this book might prove more misleading than helpful and so those wishing to reach the walks by bus are advised to obtain up-to-date information by telephoning Oxfordshire County Council's Public Transport Section on 01865–810405.

All the walks described here follow public rights of way, use recognised permissive paths or cross public open space. As the majority of walks cross land used for economic purposes such as agriculture, forestry or the rearing of game, walkers are urged to follow the Country Code at all times:

- Guard against all risk of fire
- Fasten all gates
- Keep dogs under proper control
- Keep to the paths across farmland
- Leave no litter – take it home
- Safeguard water supplies
- Protect wild life, wild plants and trees
- Go carefully on country roads on the right-hand side facing oncoming traffic
- Respect the life of the countryside

Observing these rules helps prevent financial loss to landowners and damage to the environment, as well as the all-too-frequent bad feeling towards walkers in the countryside.

While it is hoped that the special maps provided with each walk will assist the user to complete the walks without going astray and skeleton details of the surrounding road network are given to enable walkers to shorten the routes in emergency, it is always advisable to take an Ordnance Survey map with you to enable you to shorten or otherwise vary the routes without using roads or get your bearings if you do become lost. Details of the appropriate maps are given in the introduction to each walk.

As for other equipment, readers are advised that some mud will normally be encountered on most walks particularly in woodland or shady green lanes except in the driest weather. However walking boots are to be recommended at all times, as, even when there are no mud problems, hard ruts or rough surfaces make the protection given by boots to the ankles desirable. In addition, as few Oxfordshire paths are heavily used, overgrowth is prevalent around stiles and hedge gaps particularly in summer. To avoid resultant discomfort to walkers, protective clothing is therefore always advisable.

In order to assist in co-ordinating the plans and the texts, all the numbers of paths used have been shown on the plans and incorporated into the texts. These numbers consist of the official County Council footpath number with prefix letters used to indicate the parish concerned. It is therefore most helpful to use these when reporting any path problems you may find, together, if possible, with the national grid reference for the precise location of the trouble spot, as, in this way, the problem can be identified on the ground with a minimum of time loss in looking for it. National grid references can, however, only be calculated with the help of Ordnance Survey Landranger or Pathfinder maps and an explanation of how this is done can be found in the Key to all Landranger maps.

The length of time required for any particular walk depends on a number of factors such as your personal walking speed, the number of hills, stiles, etc. to be negotiated, whether or not you stop to rest, eat or drink, investigate places of interest, etc. and the number of impediments such as mud, crops, overgrowth, ploughing, etc. you encounter, but generally an average speed of between two and two and a half miles per hour is about right. It is, however, always advisable to allow extra time if you are limited by the daylight or catching a particular bus or train home in order to avoid your walk developing into a race against the clock.

Should you have problems with any of the paths used on the walks or find that the description given is no longer correct, the author would be most grateful if you could let him have details (c/o The Book Castle), so that attempts can be made to rectify the problem or the text can be corrected at the next reprint. Nevertheless, the author hopes that you will not encounter any serious problems and have pleasure from following the walks.

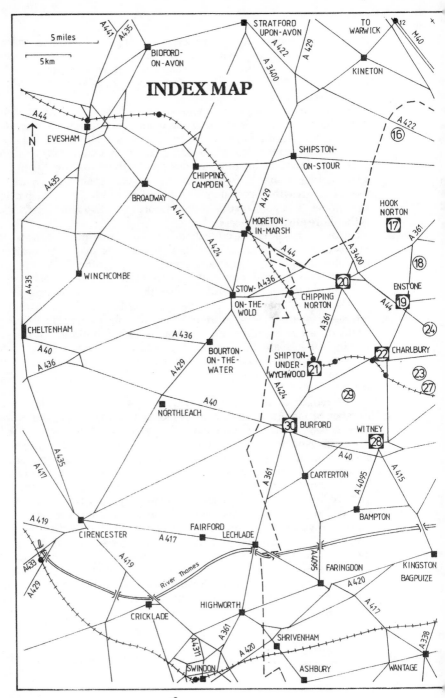

INDEX MAP

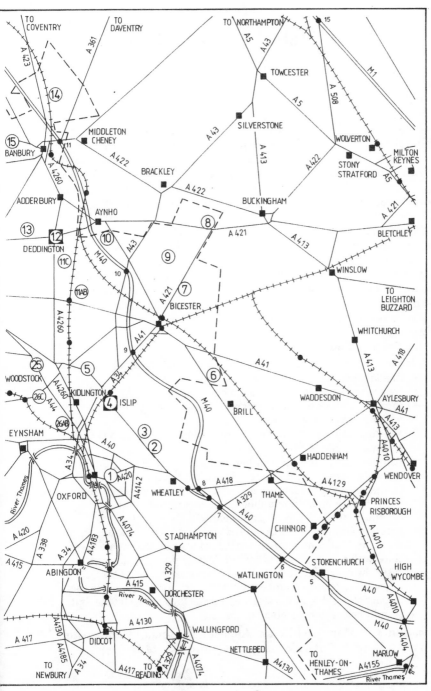

OXFORD FIELDPATHS SOCIETY

History

On the initiative of a number of people concerned about the increased use of the motor car on the footpaths in the countryside around Oxford, a meeting was held on 26th January 1926 'to form a Society for the preservation of Footpaths, Bridlepaths, and Commons in the neighbourhood of Oxford. Unless something is done to protect these, many of them will fall out of use and be forgotten. The ordinary road has more and more become either dangerous or disagreeable for the pedestrian, hence the preservation of the footpaths and bridlepaths is more necessary than ever. The latter are generally safer, quieter, and pleasanter than modern roads and brings one into much closer touch with the real country'.

The Society duly came into being, and over the years has worked constantly to protect and improve the network of public rights of way, not only in the countryside immediately around Oxford, but across the whole of the county of Oxfordshire. The Society today faces problems similar to those of 1926, but in many ways much more acute, as a result of the construction of new roads, industrial and housing developments and intensive farming.

What the Society does

Through its Executive Committee elected at the Annual General Meeting, the Society:

- makes representations to and co-operates with the appropriate local authorities on the maintenance, signposting, and waymarking of rights of way
- submits claims with documentary evidence for additions to the Definitive Map of Rights of Way
- considers all proposals for alterations to rights of way, but resisting change unless there is significant public benefit
- co-operates with other amenity societies on the above matters
- owns tools which are available to members and other organisations for path clearance work
- arranges a programme of organised walks which is sent to all members. Walks are normally on Saturdays. The starting point of some walks can be reached by public transport, but in most cases the four Oxford Park & Ride car parks are used for car-sharing to help members without cars and to minimise the impact of parking at the starting point. Dogs are welcome, but should be kept on a lead at all times.

Application for Membership to: Anneke Siertsema, Membership Secretary, 21 Rowles Close, Kennington, Oxford OX1 5LX

WALK 1 : OXFORD (ST. CLEMENT'S)

Length of Walk: (A) 8.4 miles / 13.5 Km
(B) 7.2 miles / 11.7 Km
Starting Point: Entrance to Headington Hill Park, St. Clement's.
Grid Ref: SP529063
Maps: OS Landranger Sheet 164
OS Pathfinder Sheets 1092 (SP41/51)
& 1116 (SP40/50)

How to get there / Parking: Headington Hill Park, 1 mile east of Carfax, may be reached from the City Centre by taking the A420 towards London over Magdalen Bridge and through St. Clement's. Some 200 yards beyond the Marston Road traffic lights turn left through ornamental gates into the unsignposted car park of Headington Hill Park. N.B. As the park gates are closed before sunset, walkers arriving less than 5 hours before closing time are advised to seek an alternative, possibly the public car park in Headington.

Notes: As the sections of the walk through Headington Hill Park, and the University Parks are closed before sunset, an alternative route using public rights of way is indicated on the plan. Flooding is possible after heavy rain on parts of the section between St. Clement's and the A40.

Oxford, which the nineteenth-century poet Matthew Arnold dubbed as the 'City of Dreaming Spires' in his 'Scholar Gipsy', received this name not only because of its architectural beauty which attracts 1.5 million tourists every year but also because of its superb landscape setting. Indeed, while the City has trebled in size since Matthew Arnold looked down on it from Boars Hill, a combination of the constraints of the river flood plains, the benevolence of some landowners and modern planning policies have ensured that areas of open country extend right to the heart of the City and so not only has the beauty of the views been preserved but numerous attractive walks remain possible from central Oxford.

St. Clement's, where this walk starts, is thought to have been established as a suburban village following the construction in 1004

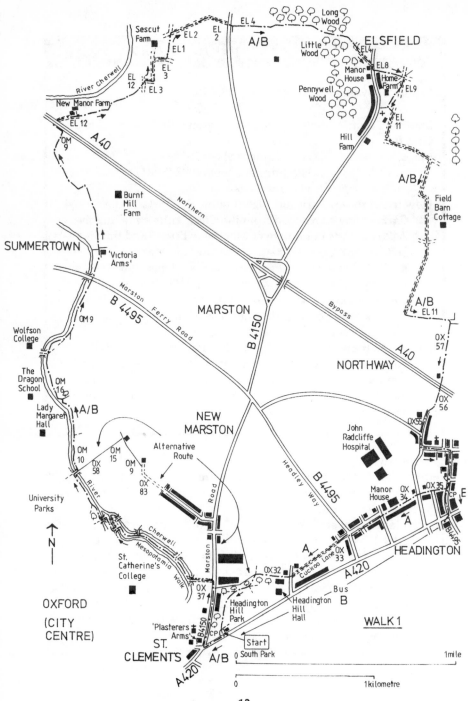

12

of a bridge called Pettypont on the site of today's Magdalen Bridge. Although it remained small for eight centuries, St. Clement's was swamped by the expansion of Oxford in the nineteenth century and formally became part of the City in 1837. Its present church was built in 1828 to replace one near Magdalen Bridge, while Headington Hill Hall, in whose former park the walk starts, was once the seat of the Morrell family, noted Oxford brewers and more recently home to the publisher Robert Maxwell.

Both walks lead you from St. Clement's along the beautiful Cherwell valley by way of Mesopotamia Walk, the University Parks and the 'Victoria Arms', one of Oxford's famous riverside inns, to the A40 and Sescut Farm before climbing to the hilltop village of Elsfield with its superb views across the City and crossing a valley to the picturesque backwater of Old Headington. Walk B then takes advantage of a frequent bus service while Walk A follows Cuckoo Lane, a normally quiet suburban path, back to Headington Hill Park.

Both walks start from the entrance to Headington Hill Park and turn right onto the A420. At the traffic lights turn right into Marston Road (B4150) passing the 'Plasterers Arms' and St. Clement's Church. After a quarter mile at the far end of a left-hand stone wall turn left onto enclosed path OX37 to the banks of the Cherwell and gates into the University Parks. Go through the gates, cross a bridge over part of the river and follow Mesopotamia Walk straight on for nearly half a mile over a series of islands. Where wooden gates block your way ahead, turn left over a bridge then right onto a gravel path to a kissing-gate. Here cross a cycle track and go through a gate opposite then turn left onto a gravel path which soon rejoins the cycle track. Having crossed another bridge, turn right through a kissing-gate onto a gravel path along the banks of the Cherwell. After a quarter mile turn right over a high arched bridge over the river leaving the University Parks.

Now turn left over a small footbridge onto path OM10 bearing left and following the riverbank through a series of meadows past the grounds of Lady Margaret Hall, the first women's college founded in 1878, on the other bank. After a third of a mile, on entering a copse where the path forks, turn left over a footbridge onto path OM16, soon rejoining the riverbank opposite the grounds of The Dragon School and following it through four meadows, part of which is a

13

nature reserve for rare meadowland flora. By a private footbridge into Wolfson College ignore a crossing path and continue along the riverbank to cross a stile by a gate. Now take path OM9 along the riverbank to Marston Ferry Road (B4495). Having crossed this road, take path OM9 straight on through scrubland to a footbridge into the grounds of the 'Victoria Arms'. Here follow the top of a slight bank bearing slightly left to pass left of the terrace wall of the inn and cross a rail-stile. Now follow the top of the bank straight on across a field to a rail-stile and footbridge. Cross these and another stile and go straight on past some poplar trees then bear slightly left to a gap in the far hedge. Here bear left to cross two sets of rails in the same hedge leading into the next field then bear left and follow a left-hand stream. At the far end of the field go through a gate then turn right through a second and cross a field diagonally to a gate left of a tall tree leading to the A40.

Turn left onto its cycle track then after some 80 yards cross the road by way of a staggered gap in the central reservation crash-barrier and take path EL12 straight on up the drive to New Manor Farm. By the farm follow a right-hand fence straight on to cross a stile into a fenced path then cross another stile and continue between hedges. On nearing a gate ahead, bear left and follow a right-hand fence then bear right beside a right-hand hedge with a view of the eighteenth-century Woodeaton Manor ahead. By a large electricity pylon bear slightly left to keep left of a hedge, then at the far end of the field cross a concealed stile and footbridge. Now turn left through an iron gate onto bridleway EL3, immediately turning right by red gates and following a fenced track round two sides of a field. On passing through a hedge gap near Sescut Farm, turn right into a green lane and look out for a footbridge in the left-hand hedge. Turn left over this onto path EL1 and follow it beside a left-hand hedge to a farm road (path EL2). Now turn right onto this and follow it, with a closer view of Woodeaton Manor to your left, to reach Woodeaton Lane. Cross this road and take fenced bridleway EL4 right of iron gates, following a right-hand hedge straight on, then continuing past Long Wood, joining a concrete road and following it uphill to Elsfield.

Here turn right onto a road then before the first left-hand cottage and the right-hand Manor House, home of the author John Buchan, later Lord Tweedsmuir, from 1919 to 1940, turn left onto a gravel drive (path EL8) to enter a field. Now go straight on uphill to a track junction at the top by the left-hand end of a hedge. Turn round here for an extensive view of the Cherwell valley then go past the end of the hedge and turn right onto path EL9 following a right-hand hedge. After some 70 yards turn right over a concealed stile under a walnut tree and cross a field diagonally passing just left of a stone granary to reach a stile at the back of Elsfield churchyard where John Buchan is buried near the thirteenth-century church. Do NOT cross this stile but turn left onto path EL11 bearing half right across a corner of the field to cross a stile. Here turn right onto a grassy track and follow it downhill beside a right-hand fence with a view of Headington dominated by the John Radcliffe Hospital ahead, eventually bearing left to reach a T-junction of tracks. Here go left following a track beside a left-hand hedge over a rise with a panoramic view over Oxford to your right. Where the track forks, turn right crossing the field. At its far hedge, still following the track, turn left then right and continue across three fields ignoring a crossing track then following a right-hand hedge. At the far end of the third field by a hedge and stream marking the city boundary, turn left and follow them nearly to the far side of the field to reach a concrete footbridge. Turn right over this and a stile then take path OX57 beside a right-hand hedge across two fields to reach the A40 Oxford Northern Bypass. Cross this dual-carriageway carefully then take enclosed bridleway OX56 straight on, starting to climb and widening into a road (byway OX55) and eventually reaching a T-junction in Old Headington.

Headington today is an important suburban centre, but prior to its incorporation into Oxford City in 1929 it was a large independent parish. Recorded as a royal manor in Saxon times, Headington expanded after the London turnpike road, which had formerly crossed Shotover Plain, was rerouted past the village in 1775. This eventually led to its centre moving from the old village to the turnpike road (now the A420) and for this reason Old Headington with its fine Norman church and attractive stone inns and cottages has now become a quiet backwater retaining its rural atmosphere.

At the T-junction bear slightly left into St. Andrew's Road and follow it bearing left past the church and the 'White Hart' then turn right into Old High Street. **Walk B** now follows this straight on to the traffic lights on the A420 where you cross the main road, turn right for the bus stop and take a bus back to your starting point. **Walk A** also follows Old High Street for some 300 yards then, about 40 yards before the entrance to a left-hand car park, turns right into Cuckoo Lane (path OX35), a narrow alley passing under an archway. Follow this, crossing a road and (now as OX34) passing The Manor football ground (due to close in 1998) and the grounds of the Manor House to reach a second road. Cross this, pass between anti-cycle rails and follow a macadam path beside Woodlands Road to Headley Way (B4495). Having crossed this, take Woodlands Road straight on then, at a right-hand bend, leave the road and take Cuckoo Lane (now OX33) straight on between bollards. On nearing a road called Pullen's Lane, bear left beside the left-hand wall then cross the road by a white gate and take path OX32 virtually opposite noting a boundary stone dated 1901 in the right-hand hedge. After some 250 yards where the left-hand stone wall ends, turn left through a gate in iron railings into Headington Hill Park and take a gravel path. At a junction bear slightly right onto a wide macadam path and follow it straight on, ignoring a branching path to the right, to reach the car park.

WALK 2 : STANTON ST. JOHN

Length of Walk:	6.6 miles / 10.6 Km
Starting Point:	Stanton St. John Village Hall.
Grid Ref:	SP578093
Maps:	OS Landranger Sheet 164
	OS Pathfinder Sheet 1116 (SP40/50)

How to get there / Parking: Stanton St. John, 4.5 miles northeast of Oxford, may be reached from the Headington Roundabout, the junction of the A40, A420 and A4142, by taking Bayswater Road (signposted to the Crematorium, Stanton St. John, etc.) through Barton Estate. Where open country begins to your right, turn right onto the road signposted to Stanton St. John, Oakley and Brill. At a T-junction with the B4027 turn right then immediately left onto a road into the village. By the church fork right looking out for the village hall car park after some 70 yards on your left.

Stanton St. John, like many villages on Oxford college estates, has a number of fine stone houses, some of sixteenth-century origin, and a twelfth-century church with a buttressed tower and fine screenwork from the fifteenth century. The manor, once belonging to a monastic order, has, since the Reformation, been the property of New College and even today the College owns much of the local land. In 1575 the village was the birthplace of John White, later a Fellow of New College, best known as one of the Pilgrim Fathers and chief founder in 1624 of the colony of Massachusetts. At about the same time it was also home to the grandfather of the poet John Milton, a yeoman farmer and ranger to the Royal Forest of Shotover.

The walk with its series of superb views explores the scenic hill country to the east and south of the village which, unlike much of Oxfordshire, is liberally interspersed with woodland, the remains of the ancient royal forests of Bernwood and Shotover. Having skirted the scattered village of Holton, you then cross the A40 to enjoy the beautiful parkland of Shotover House before returning by way of the rural hillside village of Forest Hill, scene in 1643 of John Milton's wedding, to his grandfather's home of Stanton St. John.

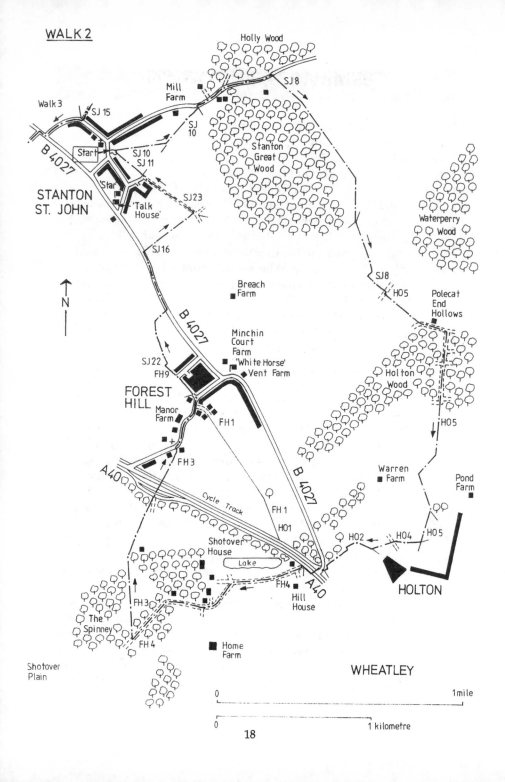

WALK 2

Holly Wood

Mill Farm

Walk 3

SJ 15

SJ 10

Start

SJ 10
SJ 11

'Star'

STANTON
ST. JOHN

'Talk House'

SJ 23

SJ 16

N

Stanton
Great
Wood

SJ 8

Waterperry
Wood

SJ 8
HO5

Polecat
End
Hollows

Breach
Farm

Minchin
Court
Farm
'White Horse'
Vent Farm

B 4027

SJ 22

FH 9

FOREST
HILL

Manor
Farm

FH 1

FH 3

A40

Holton
Wood

HO5

Warren
Farm

Pond
Farm

Cycle Track

FH 1
HO1

Shotover
House

Lake

B 4027

HO2   HO4   HO5

A40

HOLTON

FH 4

Hill
House

FH 3

The
Spinney

FH 4

Home
Farm

WHEATLEY

Shotover
Plain

0   1mile

0   1 kilometre

18

Starting from the stile at the back of Stanton St. John Village Hall car park, take path SJ10 straight down the hill to a footbridge left of two electricity poles then bear half left to cross a footbridge and stile right of a hedge corner. Here follow a powerline straight on for some 300 yards to reach gates in the left-hand hedge leading to the Menmarsh road. Turn right onto this road and follow it, later beside Holly Wood, for a third of a mile. Having rounded a left-hand bend, turn right through a black iron gate onto path SJ8 bearing slightly left across a field to a corner of Stanton Great Wood. Now follow the edge of the wood straight on to cross a culvert into the next field. Here leave the edge of the wood and aim for distant farm buildings at Polecat End Hollows to reach a footbridge over a ditch then take the alignment of the bridge straight on to cross another footbridge. Now follow a left-hand ditch with a view of Forest Hill to your right, turning right by a willow tree then left over a culvert. Continue beside a left-hand ditch to a bridlegate and sleeper bridge into a bridleway called Polecat Lane, part of an ancient road from Oxford to Thame.

Cross this lane and a stile by a gate opposite then take path HO5 beside a right-hand hedge to a corner of Holton Wood. Here bear slightly left onto a track past the farm buildings at Polecat End Hollows to a red gate into Holton Wood. Turn right through this gate and take a fire-break straight on through the wood. At the far side of the wood keep straight on, crossing a track and heading just left of a flat-roofed building at Holton to reach a fence gap. Here bear slightly right to cross stepping stones and a stile left of an oak tree then go straight on to go through a gap in the corner of a hedge. Now follow a right-hand hedge to the far end of the field then bear slightly right across the next field to the corner of a hedge. Here turn right onto path HO4 crossing the field to a gate in the right-hand hedge. Now keep straight on, crossing a raised farm road 10 yards left of a telegraph pole and continuing to a field corner. Ignore a gate in the left-hand hedge and cross a low barbed-wire fence in a gap in the right-hand hedge then follow a left-hand hedge. At the far end of the field turn left through a gate then right beside a right-hand hedge. On nearing the A40, turn right through a hedge gap onto its cycle track and cross first the mouth of the B4027 then the A40 dual-carriageway via a staggered gap in the central reservation crash-barrier. (N.B. If heavy traffic should make it impossible to cross the A40, alternative routes to Forest Hill via path HO1/FH1 or the A40 cycle track omitting the section through Shotover Park are indicated on the map.)

When crossing the A40 today, it is hard to believe that till 1775, when the London–Oxford turnpike was diverted to avoid the steep hills up to Shotover Plain, the section of the A40 between the B4027 and Forest Hill did not exist and the B4027, possibly a Roman road which had then become the London–Worcester turnpike, continued diagonally across the present A40 into Wheatley. Indeed up to about that time most travellers heading for Witney and beyond used the Worcester turnpike in preference to the Oxford turnpike to avoid the notoriously bad road over Wytham Hill and the ford at Swinford.

On reaching the far verge of the A40, turn right along it. After about 100 yards turn left through a large red gate onto bridleway FH1a, a macadam drive to Shotover House. Ignore a stile to your left and follow the drive through Shotover Park for a third of a mile with views through the trees to your right of an ornamental lake and the early eighteenth-century Palladian house built in Headington stone by General James Tyrell. By a cottage fork left onto a fenced stone track with views to your left of Home Farm, an example of an advanced industrialised Victorian farm and more views through the trees to your right of Shotover House. By the corner of a stone wall ignore a branching drive to your right then, after some 50 yards, ignore the drive to Home Farm to your left and take a rough fenced track straight on uphill. On reaching a fine avenue mainly of lime trees, glance to your right for a view of a classical temple then turn left along the avenue with fine views to your left towards Wheatley Church and the Chiltern escarpment beyond.

After 380 yards turn right over a concealed stile near a red gate onto path FH3 bearing half right across a field with views towards Stanton St. John and Otmoor passing just right of some Scots pines to cross a stile right of a red gate in the bottom corner of the field. Here bear half right to keep just left of a fenced clump of trees then pass between the right-hand pair of a group of four oaks and continue to a gate and cattle grid leading to an A40 layby. Go straight on across the layby, step over a crash-barrier and cross the main road. At the far side cross some rails by a gate and take path FH3 straight on uphill to cross a stile just right of Forest Hill Church. Now continue past a garage to reach the village street opposite the church.

Forest Hill, referred to as 'Fostel' in the Domesday Book, may derive its name from the ancient forest of Shotover, which formed its southern boundary till disafforestation in 1660. Despite its close proximity to Oxford and being sandwiched between the A40 and the B4027, much of the village retains its timeless rural charm. The church, first recorded in 1149 as a chapel-of-ease to Stanton St. John, was remodelled in the thirteenth century and dedicated to St. Nicholas in 1273 which may be when parish status was attained. It was here that in 1643 John Milton married the seventeen-year-old Mary Powell whose father lived in the village and owed Milton money.

Turn right onto this road and follow it for a quarter mile passing Manor Farm with its tall chimneys and mullioned windows rebuilt by Lincoln College in 1854 using the stone from the old house. Just past the village hall turn left onto bridleway FH8, a rough track leading to a gate. Now take path FH9 straight on beside the right-hand hedge through two fields with views to your left towards Shotover Hill, the John Radcliffe Hospital and Wytham Hill. In the second field ignore a stile into a housing estate and the first stile into the recreation ground then turn right over a rail stile into the recreation ground. Now turn left onto path SJ22 following the left-hand hedge through the recreation ground and the next field with fine views to your right towards Brill. Where the hedge bears left, turn right across the field to a hedge gap onto the B4027 at the near end of a line of trees. Turn left onto its footway and after a quarter mile just before a small gas installation to your right, turn right across the road and stile onto path SJ16 with panoramic views towards Otmoor, the Brill hills and the Chilterns. Now head for Brill and a hedge separating two fields in front of Stanton Great Wood to reach the near end of this hedge. Here turn left onto bridleway SJ23, a grassy track towards Stanton St. John Church. By the end of an estate road take path SJ11 straight on over a stile by a gate then downhill and up again to the stile into the village hall car park.

Length of Walk:	6.5 miles / 10.5 Km
Starting Point:	'Abingdon Arms', Beckley
Grid Ref:	SP565112
Maps:	OS Landranger Sheet 164
	OS Pathfinder Sheets 1092 (SP41/51)
	& 1116 (SP40/50)

How to get there / Parking: Beckley, 4.5 miles northeast of
Oxford, may be reached from the Headington Roundabout,
the junction of the A40, A420 and A4142, by taking
Bayswater Road (signposted to the Crematorium,
Stanton St. John, etc.) straight on for 1.7 miles to the B4027.
Turn left onto this, then after 200 yards turn right onto the
road to Beckley. In the village follow the priority road
bearing right by the church into High Street. Where the
road widens, look for a suitable parking space, but do *not*
use the pub car park without the landlord's permission.

Notes: Some low-lying paths used may be waterlogged or
heavy-going after wet weather.

Beckley on a high ridge overlooking the flat lowlands of Otmoor is
today probably best known for its tall radio and television mast
which can be seen for miles around, but this picturesque village of
stone cottages on a loop road seldom used by through-traffic has, in
fact, through the ages been a place of some importance. The largest
of the 'seven towns of Otmoor' at the time of the Norman conquest,
Beckley is sited on the Roman road from Dorchester to Alchester
(near Wendlebury) and the remains of a small Roman villa have
been found nearby, while its church, originally Norman, but largely
rebuilt in the fourteenth century, has a number of wall paintings
and its original stone tub font. In the Middle Ages the manor, which
had reputedly once belonged to King Alfred who may have built
the moats at Beckley Park, was held by a succession of national
figures including Robert D'Oilly, Piers Gaveston and Lord
Williams of Thame and can boast the site of a palace. In more recent
times, the noted writers R D Blackmore and John Buchan, both of

whom lived in nearby Elsfield, set books in the village, Evelyn Waugh lived for a time at the 'Abingdon Arms' and Lewis Carroll (the pen-name of the Oxford don, Charles Dodgson) is believed to have taken the view of Otmoor from the village as the inspiration for his chess game in 'Alice through the Looking Glass'.

The walk explores the beautiful hill country to the northeast of Oxford with its scattering of woods remaining from the ancient forests of Shotover and Bernwood, first leading you eastwards out of Beckley with spectacular views across Otmoor and towards the distant Chilterns before descending to the edge of the moor near Horton-cum-Studley. You now turn south skirting woodland and climbing to Stanton St. John with more fine views before continuing towards the edge of Oxford, then turning north again and following a route on or close to the Roman road back by way of Stowood to Beckley.

Starting with your back to the 'Abingdon Arms', turn left taking High Street straight on at a fork. Where the public road turns sharp left into Otmoor Lane (part of the Roman road), take path BE4 (part of the Oxfordshire Way) straight on up a sunken lane to Fletchers Farm. Now keep straight on to a gate into a field where wide views open out across Otmoor to your left and towards Horton-sum-Studley backed by Muswell Hill and Brill Hill ahead. Here take a grassy track straight on past the site of the Roman villa. Where the track bears slightly right, leave it and go straight on across two fields to a stile in a hedge. Now bear slightly left along a worn path aiming towards tall conifers on the hilltop at Studley Priory at first, then gradually bearing right with views of the Chiltern escarpment to your right and Beckley Park to your left to cross a stile in the far corner of the field.

The present Beckley Park was built as a hunting lodge by Lord Williams of Thame in about 1540 and is noted for its fine diapered brickwork and stone mullioned windows. It is surrounded by three rectangular moats which may have been constructed by King Alfred who is thought to have had a hunting lodge on this site.

Now follow an enclosed path through a belt of trees to a footbridge and stile onto a farm road. Turn left onto this then immediately right through a kissing-gate by a field gate and right again over a footbridge into a marshy field on the edge of Otmoor. The moor became notorious because of riots which took place following its enclosure in 1830 and continued sporadically for five years. The enclosure of the moor and associated drainage works were, however, not totally successful as much of it has remained waterlogged, but despite or because of its wildness it has, over the years, survived plans to build railways and motorways across it and to turn it into a reservoir! Now bear half left across the field to a hunt jump in the next fence then continue to a hunt jump, gate and stiles in the far corner of the next field. Having crossed these, bear half right across a large marshy field to a yellow gate and stile in the next hedge then bear slightly right to cross a footbridge and stile. Here take path HS5 following the left-hand hedge to a stile then bear half right across the next field to a stile in the far corner onto the Horton-cum-Studley road.

Cross this road and take bridleway HS6 through a gateway opposite then follow a left-hand hedge. Near the far end of the field leave the hedge and bear slightly right across the field corner to cross a gated bridge. Now bear slightly right across the next field to a wide hedge gap by a corner of Stanton Little Wood. Enter this hedge gap, but before reaching a culvert, leave the Oxfordshire Way turning right onto path HS16, a green lane along the edge of the wood and following it for over a third of a mile to rejoin the Horton-cum-Studley road.

Turn left onto this road then after 100 yards turn left again onto bridleway SJ2, a gated concrete, later stone track leading to an underground gas installation. Near this installation pass left of its gate and follow a fenced track past the compound to enter a field. Bear half right across the field to a corner of a hedge then turn right onto path SJ13 heading for a tree left of both a hedge junction in the next dip and Woodperry House on a hilltop. By the tree cross a footbridge and bear half right crossing a stile and continuing uphill to cross a stile in the left-hand hedge left of the first of two oak trees. Now turn right onto a grass track and go through a hedge gap then turn left onto another grass track. Where the track turns left through a hedge gap, leave it and follow the right-hand side of the hedge gradually bearing right with wide views to your left towards Forest Hill and the distant Chilterns beyond. On reaching a corner of the field go straight on over wooden rails then turn right onto path SJ14, a grassy track beside a right-hand hedge. After 150 yards turn left onto bridleway SJ15, another grassy track following a left-hand hedge. On reaching a gate

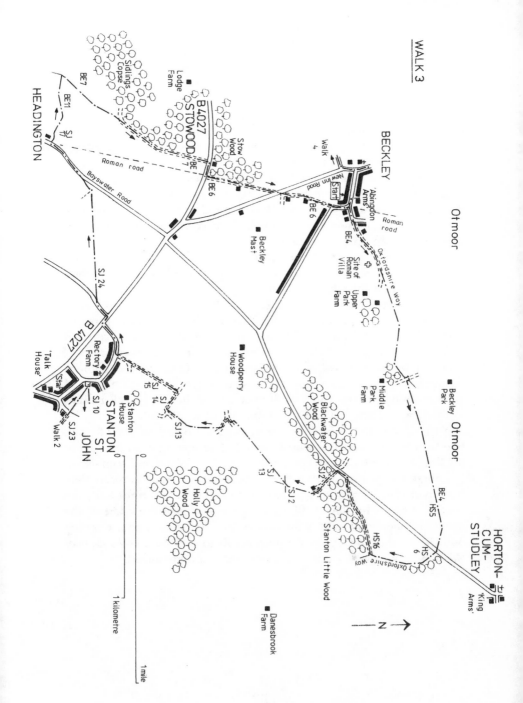

25

and gap onto a macadam drive, join the drive and take it straight on to a road on the edge of Stanton St. John (described in Walk 2).

Turn right onto this road and follow it to the B4027. Here turn right then immediately left onto the Headington and Oxford road. After 130 yards, where the right-hand hedge begins, turn right through a former gateway onto path SJ24 bearing half left across the field with fine views of Shotover Hill to your left, to cross a stile and footbridge between the second and third pylons from the left of a distant powerline. Now bear half left across the corner of a field to cross a concealed footbridge then bear half right across the next field to go through a hedge gap with a low wooden rail in the far corner. Now turn left along a wide scrubby roadside verge, eventually reaching Bayswater Road near the edge of Oxford.

Turn left onto this road and follow it towards Oxford. Just before houses begin to your right and the road joins the line of the Roman road, turn right through a gap by an iron gate onto path SJ17 (later BE11) following a left-hand hedge for a third of a mile, later with glimpses to your left of the John Radcliffe Hospital and spires of Oxford backed by Cumnor Hill. At the far end of the field turn right onto formerly fenced bridleway BE7 and follow it for three-quarters of a mile, later with views to your right of Red Hill and the Chiltern escarpment beyond, then widening into a farm track, passing a wood and continuing to the B4027 at Stowood opposite Royal Oak House, formerly a coaching inn on the London–Worcester turnpike.

Turn right onto the B4027 verge passing the house, then by an oak tree turn left onto enclosed bridleway BE6 following it on the line of the Roman road for a third of a mile past Stow Wood and some farm buildings and passing within 350 yards of Beckley Mast to reach New Inn Road. Turn left onto this road then immediately right onto the continuation of bridleway BE6 taking the enclosed track left of the drive to 'Meonwara' with views across Beckley and Otmoor opening out ahead, then dropping through scrub to a bend in Woodperry Road in Beckley where your starting point is straight ahead.

WALK 4 :   ISLIP

Length of Walk: (A) 8.4 miles / 13.5 Km
                  (B) 5.0 miles / 8.0 Km
Starting Point: Public car park opposite the 'Swan Inn', Islip.
Grid Ref: SP528140
Maps: OS Landranger Sheet 164
                  OS Pathfinder Sheet 1092 (SP41/51)
How to get there / Parking: Islip, 5 miles north of Oxford, may be
    reached from the Peartree Roundabout on the Oxford Ring
    Road by taking the A34 towards Northampton for 3.5 miles
    to its junction with the B4027. Now take the B4027 into Islip.
    In the village, after descending a narrow one-way hill, turn
    left for the public car park opposite the 'Swan Inn'.
Notes: This walk is not to be recommended after wet weather,
    as it crosses some very heavy arable fields and path IS7 is
    prone to flooding by the River Cherwell.

Islip, near the confluence of the Rivers Ray and Cherwell, has
historically been a place of some importance due to its being the
only point at which the Ray could be crossed between the Cherwell
and the fens of Otmoor. This fact led to the London–Worcester
turnpike road (the modern B4027) being routed through the village
and the consequent opening of inns to service the stagecoaches. Its
importance, however, predates the turnpike road as it was the site of
a Saxon royal palace where King Edward the Confessor was born in
1004 and its mill on the Cherwell demolished in 1939 dated from
this period. In the Civil War, Islip also was the scene of three battles
in Parliament's attempt to capture the Royalist stronghold of
Oxford. Even today, though thankfully bypassed by the M40 and
A40, the hillside village with its fine stone cottages clustered
around its mainly fourteenth-century church and small market
place still testifies to its former wealth.

Both walks cross the River Ray and explore the low range of hills
to the southeast separating Otmoor from the Cherwell valley and
Oxford which formerly was part of Shotover Forest, visiting Noke
on the edge of the Moor and the small village of Woodeaton. In so

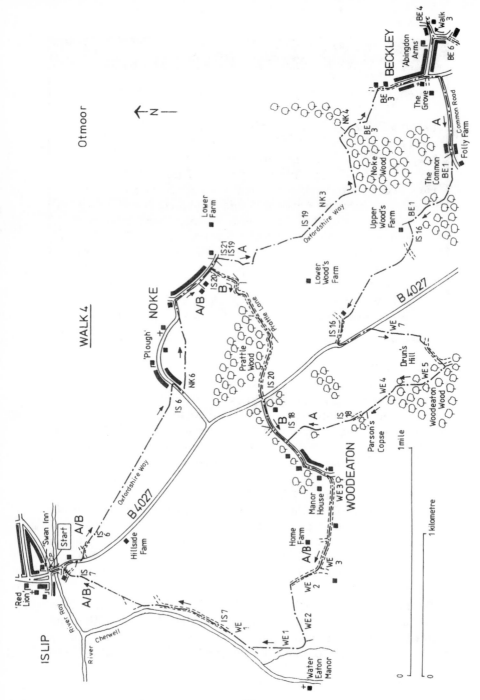

WALK 4

Otmoor

ISLIP

NOKE

BECKLEY
'Abingdon Arms'

WOODEATON

28

doing, they also offer superb views both across Otmoor towards the Brill hills and along the Cherwell valley towards Oxford. Walk A additionally visits the ancient hilltop village of Beckley with its picturesque cottages and panoramic viewpoints.

Walks A and B start from the public car park opposite the 'Swan Inn' in Islip and take the B4027 over the River Ray bridge and uphill out of the village. Just past the speed delimiter sign, turn left over a stile left of a gate onto path IS6 (part of the Oxfordshire Way) crossing a concrete road and following a grassy track diagonally across the allotments to a gate and stile. Here follow a right-hand hedge straight on to a further stile, then keep straight on across three fields with fine views to your left towards Muswell Hill and Brill Hill and over your left shoulder towards Islip. Now cross a stile by an ash tree and bear slightly left across the fourth field to a clump of bushes on the skyline where there are fine views to your left towards Oddington and Charlton-on-Otmoor beyond and behind you towards Islip and Kidlington Church beyond. Here cross a stile, go through some bushes and follow a left-hand hedge downhill to a further stile into a hedged path leading to Noke village street.

Noke, one of the 'seven towns of Otmoor' whose inhabitants fought a bitter but unsuccessful campaign in the 1830s against the inclosure of the Moor, is today a sleepy cul-de-sac village with thatched stone cottages and farms. Part of its tiny church dates from the eleventh century having been built by Gundrada, daughter of William the Conqueror.

Turn right onto this road and follow it uphill for 100 yards then at a slight right-hand bend, turn left over a stile onto path NK6 following the left-hand edge of the field downhill to cross a footbridge and stile. Now bear slightly left across the next field to a hedge gap leading to a bend in Noke village street. Turn right onto this, then at a fork, turn right again.

After a quarter mile, opposite the gates to a house called Lower Valley, **Walk B** turns right onto bridleway IS20 and follows this winding green lane known as Prattle Lane for over two-thirds of a mile, soon skirting Prattle Wood, to reach the B4027. Cross this road and take Woodeaton Lane straight on soon rejoining **Walk A**. Now omit the next four paragraphs.

Walk A continues to the end of the public road, then takes bridleway IS21 straight on over a concrete culvert before turning right over a stile onto path IS19 (still the Oxfordshire Way). Now follow the right-hand hedge and stream with a fine view towards Beckley with its TV mast on a hilltop ahead. At a field corner turn left, still beside the right-hand hedge and stream with views of Muswell Hill and Brill Hill ahead, soon bearing right and continuing for half a mile to reach Noke Wood. Now on path NK3 turn left and follow a ditch along the edge of the wood with fine views to your left across Otmoor towards Oddington, Charlton-on-Otmoor and Graven Hill, eventually turning right to reach a corner of the field. Here take path NK4 straight on over a culvert and through Noke Wood. At the far side of the wood cross another culvert and bear half right onto fenced path BE3 following a left-hand hedge uphill then turning left over a stile into a field. Here bear half right across two fields to cross a stile into Church Lane, Beckley at the far right-hand corner of the second field. Now follow this green lane, later a village street uphill past some fine stone cottages to a road junction near the church.

Beckley, on its commanding ridge above Otmoor, had a series of prominent mediaeval lords of the manor including Robert D'Oilly and Piers Gaveston and also has several literary connections with Evelyn Waugh having lived at the 'Abingdon Arms' and John Buchan and R D Blackmore setting their 'The Blanket of the Dark' and 'Cripps the Carrier' in the village. The predominantly fourteenth-century church has a number of wall paintings and a stone tub font dating from about 1200.

Now fork right onto the priority road and follow it uphill out of the village. At a further road junction turn right into Common Road passing a fine Georgian stone manor house to your right. After a third of a mile go past a thatched cottage, then opposite a cottage called Hewel Barn turn right through a bridlegate. Now fork left onto path BE1 passing right of a lime tree and left of a sunken area of trees and bushes, then bear slightly right to the bottom corner of the field. Here ignore a small gate into a copse ahead and bear right through a New Zealand (barbed-wire) gate. Bear slightly left into a field then right to follow the edge of a belt of trees. At the far end of the trees bear slightly left downhill to cross a stile and footbridge in the bottom corner of the field. Now turn left onto bridleway IS16 following a left-hand hedge. At a corner of the field cross a farm drive and go straight on through a gap left of a gate, following a left-hand hedge to a bridge and gate at the far end of the field. Here bear slightly left across the next field to pass left of a new farm. Just past the farm turn right through a gateway then left onto a rough farm road to reach the B4027.

Turn left onto this road and follow it round a left-hand bend. Where its right-hand hedge gives way to a tree belt, turn right onto path WE7 following a short green lane to a New Zealand gate into a field. Go straight on across the field to join a right-hand hedge at a corner and follow it for some 300 yards looking out for a stile and footbridge to your right. Cross these and turn left following a left-hand hedge then a grassy track past an orchard to the edge of Woodeaton Wood. Here go straight on through a gap into the wood, then turn right onto path WE5 following the inside edge of the wood for a quarter mile to cross a stile into a field near the site of a lost farm. Now take path WE4 straight on, at first walking parallel to the edge of the wood to your left, to reach the corner of the bottom hedge right of an electricity pole. Bear half left beside a right-hand hedge to a corner of the field, then slightly right into a short green lane between a copse and a hedge. On entering a field, take path IS18 straight on to an oak tree in the middle then bear half right to pass through a gap at a wiggle in the right-hand hedge. Now follow a left-hand hedge uphill to a gate into Woodeaton Lane, where you turn left rejoining Walk B.

Walks A and B now take Woodeaton Lane into Woodeaton. At a left-hand bend before the thirteenth-century church with a fourteenth-century mural of St. Christopher and fifteenth-century tower, turn right through a gap by a gate onto path WE3 and follow this green lane for nearly half a mile passing an eighteenth-century manor house to your right and with views towards the 'dreaming spires' of Oxford to your left. At a junction of green lanes turn right onto path WE2 following a green lane to enter a field. Here turn left following a left-hand hedge gently downhill with views of the Jacobean Water Eaton Manor and nearby chapel ahead backed by the Kidlington grain silo, the twin villages of Kidlington and Gosford slightly to your right and Oxford dominated by the modern white John Radcliffe Hospital to your left. At the bottom of the field turn right onto path WE1 following the banks of a Cherwell backwater. Where this bears left, leave it and go straight on across the field to join the far hedge concealing the main River Cherwell. Turn right and follow its banks to cross a stile, then take path IS7 following a grassy track along the riverbank. Where the track turns right and climbs steeply, leave it and go straight on over a stile with Islip Church coming into view ahead, then follow the edge of the field straight on beside the Cherwell. Where the river begins to bear left, leave it and bear half right across the field to a stile, then bear half right across the next field to a stile right of a white post. Now follow a left-hand hedge downhill through a small field and some allotments, then continue down a rough lane to the B4027 where you turn left over the River Ray bridge for your starting point.

WALK 5 :   BLETCHINGDON

Length of Walk: 7.5 miles / 12.1 Km
Starting Point: Crossroads near Bletchingdon Post Office.
Grid Ref: SP502176
Maps: OS Landranger Sheet 164
OS Pathfinder Sheet 1092 (SP41/51)
How to get there / Parking: Bletchingdon, 7 miles north of
Oxford, may be reached from the Peartree Roundabout on the
Oxford Ring Road by taking the A34 towards Northampton
for 3.5 miles to its junction with the B4027. Now take the B4027
for 1.6 miles to the crossroads at Bletchingdon village green.
Here turn left into the Hampton Poyle road and park in one
of the right-hand parking bays or residential cul-de-sacs off it.
Notes: Parts of this walk are prone to flooding by the River
Cherwell after heavy rain.

Bletchingdon (or Bletchington) is today characterised by its
picturesque stone cottages surrounding a triangular, leafy green. Its
air of serenity, however, belies its violent past as in 1596 the village
was the scene of riots in protest at Francis Poure's attempts to
complete the inclosure of the parish which was, in fact, achieved by
Sir John Lenthall in 1623. In 1645 Colonel Windebank, commander
of Bletchingdon Park, which had been fortified as part of the
defences for the Royalist stronghold of Oxford, capitulated to the
advancing Cromwell in an attempt to save his terrified wife, but as
a result he was court-martialled by Prince Rupert at Oxford and
subsequently executed. The present house in the Palladian style,
which you glimpse near the end of the walk, dates from 1782 while
the nearby church is of thirteenth-century origin with a
fifteenth-century tower and Jacobean pulpit.

The walk, which is generally of an easy nature, takes you from
the hilltop village of Bletchingdon where there are views in places
to the east, south and west, to the deserted village of Hampton Gay
and the edge of Shipton-on-Cherwell before following the Oxford
Canal with its brightly-painted narrowboats northwards to Pigeon
Lock. It then climbs gently to the stone-built hilltop village of

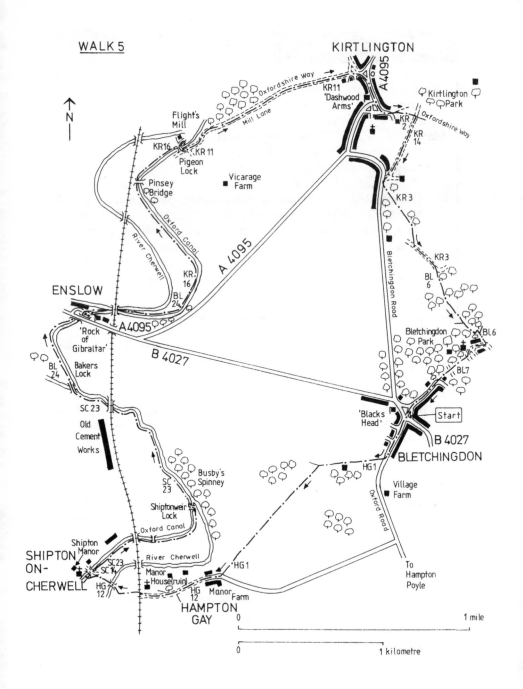

WALK 5

N

KIRTLINGTON
A 4095

Oxfordshire Way
KR11 'Dashwood Arms'
Kirtlington Park
KR 2
Oxfordshire Way
KR 14
KR 3
Flight's Mill
Mill Lane
KR16
KR 11
Pigeon Lock
Pinsey Bridge
Vicarage Farm
Oxford Canal
River Cherwell
A 4095
KR. 16
BL 24
KR3
BL 6
ENSLOW
A4095
'Rock of Gibraltar'
B 4027
Bletchingdon Road
Bletchingdon Park
BL6
Bakers Lock
BL 24
BL7
SC 23
'Blacks Head'
Start
Old Cement Works
B 4027
BLETCHINGDON
HG1
Village Farm
Busby's Spinney
SC 23
Oxford Road
Shiptonweir Lock
Oxford Canal
Shipton Manor
SC23
SC 14
River Cherwell
HG1
To Hampton Poyle
SHIPTON ON- CHERWELL
HG 12
Manor House(ruin)
HG 12
Manor Farm
HAMPTON GAY

0   1 mile

0   1 kilometre

Kirtlington before returning through Kirtlington Park and Bletchingdon Park to Bletchingdon.

Starting from the crossroads near the Post Office at Bletchingdon village green, take the Hampton Poyle road southwards to the end of the village. At the far end of the last right-hand parking bay, turn right over a stile onto path HG1 where the chimney of the former Shipton-on-Cherwell cement works comes into view ahead. Cross the field diagonally heading towards a distant copse, passing just right of some farm buildings and going through one gate, then a second about 40 yards right of a small ash tree. Now bear half right across a large field with fine views ahead on a clear day towards Kidlington with its tall church spire and Oxford, heading right of a distant treetop in the far corner of the field to reach a rail-stile in its right-hand hedge some 150 yards short of the far corner where the hamlet of Hampton Gay comes into view ahead. Now aim just right of the farmhouse of Manor Farm to go through a gate in the bottom hedge, then keep straight on across the next field passing right of an electricity pole to reach gates onto the Hampton Gay road.

Turn right onto this and follow it through the hamlet to its end. Now cross some rails by a gate onto path HG12 taking a grassy track straight on across the site of the lost village where slight mounds indicate its former buildings. Pass just left of several large chestnut trees in front of the ruins of the Jacobean manor house destroyed by fire in 1887, with the spire of Kidlington Church coming into view to your left, then continue, with the churches of Hampton Gay and Shipton-on-Cherwell coming into view to your right. Level with Hampton Gay Church which was rebuilt in 1772 but retains certain features of its predecessor such as the seventeenth-century alabaster memorial to Vincent Barry, bear half right off the track to reach a stile onto the Oxford–Banbury railway line near the site of one of the first railway disasters where thirty passengers were killed in a derailment in 1874. Cross the railway carefully then bear slightly right across meadowland passing just left of a clump of bushes and willows, then bear slightly right to cross a footbridge over the River Cherwell. Here keep straight on, crossing a stile by a gate, then continue along path SC14 towards the bridge over the Oxford Canal into Shipton-on-Cherwell.

Shipton-on-Cherwell with its large manor house and a church

rebuilt in 1831 on the banks of the Oxford Canal, constructed by James Brindley in the 1780s to link the Thames to the industrial Midlands, must once have been a sleepy rural idyll but has been somewhat spoilt by the close proximity of the former cement works and a housing estate built for some of its workers.

Do not cross this bridge, but fork left to reach the canal towpath (SC23). Turn right onto it passing under the bridge and following the east bank of the canal for over half a mile past Shipton-on-Cherwell and the bridgeheads of the old Woodstock Branch Line (opened in 1890 and closed in 1954), under a railway bridge and past a drawbridge. Eventually you reach Shiptonweir Lock where you cross a bridge to the west bank and the canal joins the Cherwell. Now follow the west bank of the river for three-quarters of a mile passing under another railway bridge near the old cement works. Where the Cherwell and the Oxford Canal again part company, cross a footbridge over the Cherwell and take path BL24 following the west bank of the canal past Bakers Lock and some moorings then under a modern bridge at Enslow carrying the A4095.

By the old road bridge cross a stile then, if wishing refreshment, turn right over this historic bridge, now preserved as a bridleway by the efforts of the Oxford Fieldpaths Society and CPRE to reach the 'Rock of Gibraltar'. Otherwise bear half right onto the continuation of path BL24 rejoining the canal bank and passing under a railway bridge. Here the Cherwell is immediately to your left for a short distance before the canal and its towpath leave it again. Now continue for a further mile (soon on path KR16) passing another drawbridge, walking under a stone bridge called Pinsey Bridge and eventually reaching Bridge No.213 at Pigeon Lock. Here go under the bridge, climb the slope at the side of the lock and turn sharp left onto a gravel road (bridleway KR11) joining the Oxfordshire Way, crossing the canal bridge then bearing left. Now follow this stone road called Mill Lane gently uphill for three-quarters of a mile past former quarries to the edge of Kirtlington.

Here take a macadam road straight on, forking right by a thatched cottage to reach the A4095. Turn right onto this and follow it to a sharp right-hand bend by the 'Dashwood Arms', then fork left (still on the Oxfordshire Way) taking a macadam road across the green. At the far corner of the green follow the road bearing slightly left (now on path KR2). Where it enters a field, leave it and follow a left-hand fence to cross a stile by a gate into Kirtlington Park. Now best known as a venue for polo matches Kirtlington Park was laid out by Capability Brown between 1751 and 1762 for Sir James Dashwood, High Sheriff of Oxfordshire, who had had its Italianate mansion (nearly half a mile to your left hidden by trees) built in 1742–6.

By the corner of the fence bear slightly right across the park heading for a wide gap in the trees ahead. On reaching a crossing stone track (path KR14), turn right onto it (leaving the Oxfordshire Way) and follow it for a quarter mile with views of Kirtlington Church to your right. Built on the site of a Saxon predecessor, this Norman church with its massive tower contains a wall painting of St. George and the dragon and the Dashwood Chapel built in 1716 with memorials to members of the family. Also buried here in 1658 was Christopher Wren, father of the famous architect who was at various times bishop of Hereford, Norwich and Ely, royal chaplain and Dean of Windsor.

On reaching a pair of gates near a stone lodge dated 1865, cross a macadam drive and go straight on to a small gate onto Bletchingdon Road. Turn left onto this and after 30 yards turn left over a concealed stile onto path KR3 bearing half right across a field to a double stile. Bear half right across the next field to join the right-hand edge of a small copse. Where the copse gives way to a hedge, cross a rail-stile then turn right and follow a right-hand hedge to a corner of the field. Here turn left onto a grassy track following a right-hand hedge. Where the track starts to bear left, turn right through a small gate onto path BL6 bearing half left across a field to a gap between two woods. Here go through a small gate into Bletchingdon Park with the house coming into view to your right then bear slightly right across the field to the corner of a fence. Follow this fence straight on, wiggling to the left at one point to reach a fenced drive. Turn right onto this (path BL7) and take it past the former stables of Bletchingdon Park and the church. By the church ignore a branching drive to your left and take a fenced stone path straight on for 300 yards to reach gates onto a bend in a road in the village, then follow this road straight on to your starting point.

WALK 6 :   PIDDINGTON (Oxon.)

Length of Walk: 6.7 miles / 10.9 Km
Starting Point: Road Junction By Piddington Church.
Grid Ref: SP640170
Maps: OS Landranger Sheet 164 or 165
OS Pathfinder Sheet 1093 (SP60/61 or
old SP61/71)

How to get there / Parking: Piddington, 5 miles southeast of
Bicester, may be reached from the southeast end of the town
by taking the A41 towards Aylesbury. After 3.2 miles turn
right onto the single track road to Piddington. Limited
parking is available at the road junction at a sharp right-hand
bend by the church. If full, return towards the A41 and park
in one of the residential cul-de-sacs to your right.

Piddington, a quiet village on the eastern edge of Oxfordshire, has
picturesque stone cottages characteristic of the county which
contrast sharply to the predominating red brick of the hilltop
village of Brill, a mere two miles away, so typical of North
Buckinghamshire. Piddington's stone church dating from around
1300 with its squat sixteenth-century tower contains a mural of St.
Christopher rediscovered in 1935 and the playwright, John
Drinkwater was buried in the churchyard in 1937. Originally a
chapel-of-ease of Ambrosden, the church replaced an early
mediaeval priory on nearby Muswell Hill where there are Iron Age
earthworks and superb panoramic views across several counties.

The walk explores the hills south of Piddington, part of the
ancient Forest of Bernwood, leading you first to the low Pans Hill
ridge with its views across the Ray and Cherwell valleys before
reaching the historical Buckinghamshire village of Boarstall. It then
takes you past Boarstall Wood to the edge of Brill before climbing
to the lofty heights of Muswell Hill and dropping down into
Piddington.

Starting from the road junction by Piddington Church, take the village
street northwards rounding a left-hand, then a right-hand bend. Just

before reaching the 'Seven Stars', turn left over a rail-stile onto path PD16. Go straight across a field passing just left of an electricity pole, with views of Muswell Hill to your left, to reach a gate in the far hedge. Now keep straight on across the next field heading just right of two tall poplars to reach the far hedge. Here turn left onto path PD15 following a right-hand hedge through two fields towards Muswell Hill. Near the far side of the second field turn right over a stile by a gate onto path PD13 and follow a right-hand hedge. At the far end of the field go straight on through the right-hand of two gates then bear slightly right across the next field to a small gate right of an oak tree. Now keep straight on to cross a stile by a gate in a corner of the field to reach the B4011.

Cross this road and take path PD13 straight on through a gate into a green lane on the edge of Piddington Wood ignoring two branching paths to your right into the wood. After a third of a mile cross a stile into a field and now on path PD21 turn right then left at a field corner and follow a right-hand hedge to the far end of the field. Crossing the Buckinghamshire boundary take path BS7 straight on through a gate, then ignore a second gate ahead and bear half right to the corner of a hedge. Follow this left-hand hedge along the Pans Hill ridge through two fields with fine views to your right across the Ray and Cherwell valleys. At the far end of the second field bear left into a corner then go through a gate and straight on across the next field towards another corner. Just short of this corner turn left through a field gate onto path BS8 going straight across a field towards the right-hand end of a wood ahead to cross two sets of rails just right of a kink in the far hedge. This wood conceals a large decoy pond constructed in the eighteenth century for catching ducks. Now bear half right to the left-hand end of a sporadic hedge where you cross a rail-stile and go straight on towards the right-hand corner of the distant Boarstall Wood, with a fine view to your left towards the hilltop village of Brill, to reach a gate. Bear half left across the next field heading for a large farmhouse. Cross a footbridge and rail-stile under two hawthorn trees then keep straight on towards a Dutch barn crossing a gated culvert and reaching a gate by the Dutch barn. Go through this gate, pass left of the barn and through a second gate, then keep straight on across a field to a rail-stile onto a road at Boarstall.

The name Boarstall is said to derive from the slaying by Niel of Boarstall of an enormous boar, the head of which he presented to

Edward the Confessor at Brill. In reward, the King is said to have knighted Niel and granted him custody of the Forest of Bernwood. This is borne out by the manor being recorded three centuries later in the hands of the Fitzniel family whose heir by marriage, Sir John de Handlo, was granted a licence to crenellate Boarstall House by King Edward II in 1312. The house, which withstood several sieges during the Civil War, finally fell to Fairfax in 1646 and much of it was demolished some years later, but the moat and fourteenth-century gatehouse known as Boarstall Tower survived and are now a National Trust property. The nearby church rebuilt in 1818 incorporates some features of its predecessor and a gate in the back wall of the churchyard permits a view of the garden on the site of Boarstall House where its foundations can still be seen.

Turn right onto the road, passing the entrance to Boarstall Tower to your right and ignoring the first left-hand path. Just past the old village school, opposite the church, turn left over a stile by a gate onto path BS1 crossing a field diagonally to a stile in the far corner. Cross this stile, a footbridge and another stile then follow a left-hand hedge with views of Muswell Hill and Brill to your left. At the far end of the field cross a stile into a small plantation and follow a winding path through it over a footbridge and on to another stile. Here turn right to a gate and stile into a field then bear half right heading right of a cottage ahead to cross a stile and footbridge. Keep straight on across the next field to a marker post about 100 yards right of the cottage. Here turn left and follow the outside edge of Boarstall Wood then the cottage hedge to a gate and stile onto the B4011.

Turn right onto this road. Just past the cottage cross the road and take path BR7 crossing a ditch and following a left-hand hedge. On joining a grassy track, bear left onto it and follow it for two-thirds of a mile along a wide green lane called Span Green to a bend in a road by Touchbridge Farm. Take this road straight on for nearly half a mile climbing the low ridge linking Muswell Hill to Brill Hill with glimpses of Brill village and its weatherboarded postmill dating from the 1680s to your right. At a crossroads turn left onto the Bicester road and follow it for half a mile up Muswell Hill with wide views opening out to your right across the Vale of Aylesbury with the prominent chimneys of Calvert Brickworks, the Ashendon Hills and the Chiltern escarpment over your right shoulder.

At the top of the hill at a left-hand bend turn right over a stile by a

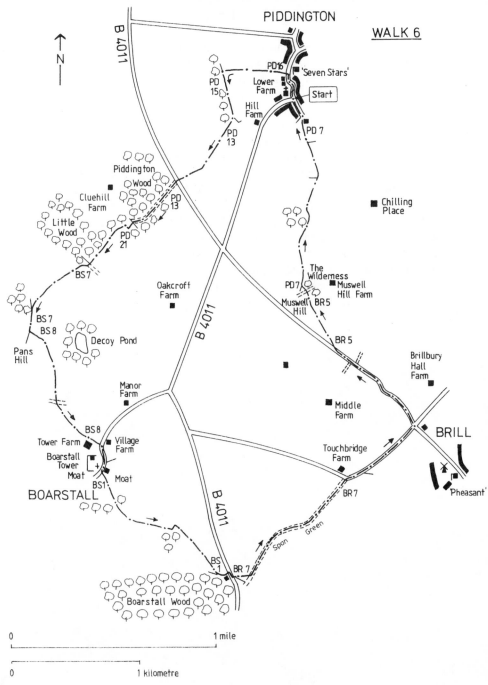

PIDDINGTON

B 4011

↑ N

'Seven Stars'

PD16

Lower Farm

Start

PD 15

Hill Farm

PD 13

PD 7

Piddington Wood

Cluehill Farm

PD 13

Little Wood

PD 21

BS 7

Chilling Place

Oakcroft Farm

The Wilderness

PD7

Muswell Hill Farm

Muswell Hill

BR5

BS 7

BS 8

Pans Hill

Decoy Pond

BR 5

Brillbury Hall Farm

Manor Farm

Middle Farm

BRILL

BS 8

Tower Farm

Village Farm

Touchbridge Farm

Boarstall Tower

Moat

Moat

Pheasant'

BS1

BOARSTALL

BR 7

B 4011

Span

Green

BS 1

BR 7

Boarstall Wood

0   1 mile

0   1 kilometre

OAKLEY

41

gate onto path BR5 with panoramic views ahead and to your right, then bear half left across the field to the left-hand end of an area of trees concealing Iron Age earthworks known as The Wilderness. On nearing the trees, wide views open out ahead across the Ray and Cherwell valleys towards the Cotswolds. Now go straight on over a stile by a gate at the county boundary and take path PD7 crossing a farm drive and a stile between the trees ahead. Here turn right and follow a right-hand fence for a third of a mile with panoramic views in virtually every direction, following the top of the ridge at first before descending steeply to cross a stile by a gate. Now follow a right-hand hedge straight on through a plantation and another field to two stiles. Cross these and bear slightly left across the next field heading towards a house with four gables to cross a stile by a gate in the far corner. Now head just right of a modern bungalow to a gate and stile leading to a fenced path and further gate and stile onto a road a Piddington, onto which you bear left for your starting point.

WALK 7 : STRATTON AUDLEY

Length of Walk:	6.9 miles / 11.1 Km
Starting Point:	Road junction by Stratton Audley Church.
Grid Ref:	SP609261
Maps:	OS Landranger Sheet 164 or 165
	OS Pathfinder Sheet 1070 (SP62/72)

How to get there / Parking: Stratton Audley, 3 miles northeast of Bicester, may be reached from the town by taking the A421 towards Buckingham. After 1.7 miles turn right onto a road signposted to Stratton Audley. At a T-junction in the village, turn right passing the 'Red Lion' and the church, then look for a suitable parking place avoiding causing obstruction or parking on mown verges.

Notes: In 1992 the route was obstructed in a number of places, but passable to the reasonably agile; however the County Council hopes to secure the elimination of the worst problems prior to publication. It may also be heavy-going after wet weather.

Stratton Audley, near the Buckinghamshire border, is named after the Roman road from Alchester to Towcester which forms the western parish boundary and the Audley family who held the manor in the Middle Ages. Near the church is indeed the site of a moated castle constructed by James Audley in the fourteenth century. The church, part of which dates from Norman times, also largely originated in this period. Despite heavy restoration in Victorian times, it retains an octagonal mediaeval font, some old glass, a Jacobean pulput and the massive tomb of Sir John Borlase, whose family took over the manor from the Audleys. The nearby Manor in part dates from the sixteenth century although much of it is more modern.

The walk, though hard-going in some conditions due to obstructions and the preponderance of arable fields, is nevertheless rewarding as it offers a number of fine views and visits the attractive village of Fringford with its spacious green, model for Flora Thompson's Candleford Green and also explores the remote tract of countryside around the deserted village of Godington.

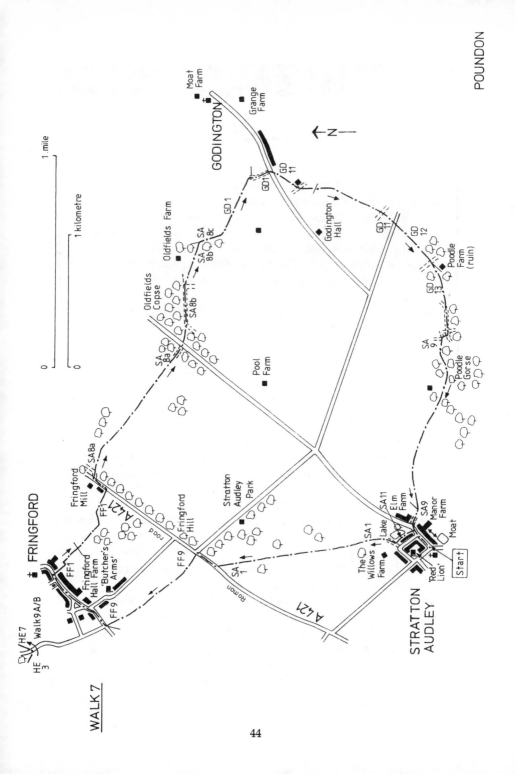

WALK 7

FRINGFORD

GODINGTON

POUNDON

STRATTON AUDLEY

44

Starting from the road junction by Stratton Audley Church and Manor, take the Poundon and Tingewick road passing Cavendish Place then, where a left-hand stone wall ends, turn left onto path SA11 following a stone wall past an attractive lake. At the far end of the lake turn right and follow grassy path SA1 between the lake and a stone wall to a gate and stile into a field. Here bear half left following a left-hand hedge to the far corner of the field. Now go through two small gates with a view of a large Victorian house called Stratton Audley Park ahead and bear half left across a field to its far corner. Cross a ditch and some wooden rails then bear half right across the next field heading just right of an electricity pole on the skyline between two copses, to cross a rail stile some 50 yards right of the far corner of the field. (If overgrown, go through the hedge gap in the field corner.) Now bear half left across the corner of the next field to a gate in the left-hand hedge, then head for the electricity pole again to pass through a gap in the next hedge and continue uphill to the pole where there is a fine view behind you towards Muswell Hill near Brill and the Chiltern escarpment beyond. Here keep straight on to reach double gates onto the A421. Turn right onto this Roman road and follow it to a road junction at Fringford Hill.

Here turn left through the right-hand of two gates onto path FF9 following a left-hand hedge to a corner of the field, then go straight on through a hedge gap and bear slightly right across a field to a gap in the next hedge. Keep straight on across the next field passing just left of an electricity pole to cross some rails and a ditch at the next hedge. Now bear slightly right across a field heading just left of a dead tree and a clump of bushes to reach a stile leading to a road junction on the edge of Fringford.

Fringford is centred on its attractive green where the authoress Flora Thompson worked at the former post office and Dr Anthony Addington, whose son Henry Addington became Prime Minister in 1805, had a house, while the heavily restored Norman church at the end of the village street contains a monument to Dr Addington.

Turn right onto the road into the village passing The Laurels. At a road junction by a chestnut tree, fork left onto a road across the village green, ignoring branching roads to the left, then take Main Street straight on. Just past Church Close and Fringford Cottage turn right over a concealed stile onto path FF1 and follow it between walls, later a fence and a stream, to a stile into a field. Now follow the left-hand hedge generally straight on through three fields to the A421. Cross this road and turn left onto its narrow verge. At a left-hand bend turn right through a gate and a belt of trees onto path SA8a. On entering a field, go straight on across it to an outcrop of the left-hand hedge, then bear half right across the field to a gap by the farthest right-hand tree in the next hedge. Here go straight on heading for an ash tree on the skyline to pass through a gap in the next hedge, then follow a left-hand hedge straight on over a hill with views of Brill Hill and Muswell Hill to your right. At the far end of the field take a fire-break straight on between plantations to reach a road.

Cross this road and a stile by gates virtually opposite, then take path SA8b straight along a wide fire-break through Oldfields Copse to a hedge gap. Here turn left onto a grassy track along the outside edge of the wood to reach a stile. Cross this and turn right, ignoring a second stile to your left and passing through a hedge gap. Now bear half left heading for the middle of a belt of poplars and willows, crossing a stile and continuing to a large footbridge over a brook. Cross this and go through a tree belt, then turn right onto path SA8c along the edge of the tree belt. Where the poplars end, bear slightly left across a corner of the field to cross a footbridge. Now take path GD1 bearing half left across a field, passing a bend in a left-hand stream which forms the Buckinghamshire boundary and continuing to a wooden gate just right of the far corner of the field. Go through this gate and over a culvert then turn right through a gate in the right-hand hedge, turning immediately left and taking a fenced grassy track uphill to a road on the edge of the scattered village of Godington.

Godington, which today consists of its church rebuilt in 1792, several farms, one of which is moated, and a few modern houses, is believed to be a 'deserted village' which was larger in mediaeval times. Although the whole parish was inclosed by agreement in 1603, it is believed that this occurred as a result of depopulation and was not the cause of it as in many other cases.

Cross this road and take path GD11 through a gate opposite bearing half right across two fields, with views to your left towards Poundon and Calvert Brickworks with its prominent chimneys and later views ahead towards Graven Hill near Bicester, and passing through a gate to reach the right-hand side of a group of willows concealing a pond by a stone building. Here cross a wooden fence and a grassy track then bear half left across the next field to a hedge gap right of a clump of willows in the bottom corner. Go through this gap and cross a ditch then bear slightly left across the next field to the right-hand of two oaks in the far hedge. Here cross some rails, a ditch and a grassy track then go straight on across a field and a stile and footbridge between two hawthorn bushes right of a small oak tree to reach the Poundon road.

Cross this road and a footbridge and stile opposite onto path GD12 bearing slightly right across a field towards the ruins of a brick barn on the site of Poodle Farm. On reaching a track, cross it bearing slightly left and passing through a hedge gap, then bear slightly right onto path GD13, gradually diverging from the left-hand hedge and crossing a plantation to a gap in the hedge ahead. (If obstructed, turn right to reach a gap at the bottom corner of the plantation, then turn left.) Here bear slightly right across the next field to join a right-hand hedge where another plantation begins, then take a grassy track between the hedge and the plantation to a footbridge. Cross this and another grassy track and take a grassy track straight on between a stream and a further plantation. Where the track starts to bear left, turn right over a footbridge then left onto a grassy track to reach a gated footbridge in the corner of the field. Go straight on over this and take path SA9 bearing slightly left to a gate in the corner of the field. Here keep straight on through scrubland to a gate into another field then bear slightly right across it to a gate in the far hedge. Go straight on across a corner of the next field to a concealed gap in a tree belt leading to a gate then continue across the next field keeping parallel to the left-hand hedge to cross a stile in a disused gate and a footbridge where a view opens out towards Stratton Audley to your left and Stratton Audley Park on a hilltop to your right. Here bear slightly left aiming between two farms ahead to reach a stile and footbridge, then bear slightly left to a stile and footbridge in the top hedge. Now bear half left across the next field heading just right of Stratton Audley Church to reach a stile left of a gate in the far corner of the field. Cross this and take a wooden walkway across a marshy area to join a concrete drive by a garage. Follow this straight on to a road, then turn left for your starting point.

WALK 8 :   FINMERE

Length of Walk: 6.8 miles / 11.0 Km
Starting Point: Road junction near Finmere Church.
Grid Ref: SP636330
Maps: OS Landranger Sheet 152
OS Pathfinder Sheet 1046 (SP63/73)

How to get there / Parking: Finmere, some 7 miles northeast of
Bicester, may be reached from the town by taking the A421
towards Buckingham to the roundabout at its junction with
the B4031 on the Finmere Bypass. Here take a road straight
on into Finmere, then, at a T-junction, turn left. After a
quarter mile by the 'Kings Head' turn right into Valley Road.
Ignore a branching road to the right then where the road
forks, park in a small parking area to your right. If full, take
the Fulwell/Westbury road and find a suitable parking place.

Finmere, on a low ridge above the Great Ouse valley in the extreme
northeast corner of Oxfordshire with Northamptonshire to the west
and Buckinghamshire to the north and east, is today best known as
the venue for a popular Sunday market. Historically too the village
would seem to have been a meeting place as it lies at the crossroads
of the Roman road between the towns of Alchester (near
Wendlebury) and Lactodorum (now Towcester) and the old main
road from Buckingham to Deddington, probably of Saxon origin,
while its fourteenth-century church with a twelfth-century font
from a predecessor points to early habitation. Unusually for
Oxfordshire, Finmere's surface water does not ultimately drain into
the Thames, while Buckingham, 3.5 miles to the east, rather than an
Oxfordshire town, provides the natural focus for village life.

The walk, which is of interest to those fascinated by lost
railways, first explores the plateau to the southwest of Finmere with
its scattering of woodland before visiting Mixbury, site of a Norman
castle. You then cross the Great Ouse valley, with wide views across
three counties, to the attractive Buckinghamshire village of
Westbury before recrossing the valley with further fine views and
returning to Finmere.

Starting from the road junction near Finmere Church, take the road signposted to Fulwell and Westbury. At the far end of the village, where the road bends right by the village pond, fork left into a macadamed lane (FN3) and follow it straight on for a quarter mile, ignoring a crossing path, to reach the B4031. Turn right onto this then after 25 yards turn left crossing the road and taking bridleway FN4 through gates into a field. Now bear half right across two fields passing under a pylon and through a hedge gap to reach the far corner of the second field. Here take a fenced track bearing right, then cross the drive to some gravel workings and follow a left-hand hedge straight on.

At the far end of the field, just before the filled cutting of the old Great Central main railway line, the last main line to be built and the first to close falling victim to Dr Beeching's 'axe' in the 1960s, turn left over a bridlebridge and take a fenced track between the gravel workings and the former railway cutting. Where a fence blocks your way ahead, turn right across the former railway then go straight on across the next field to a hedge gap left of a thatched cottage hidden by a clump of trees. Here cross a farm road and go through a gate then bear half left to a former gateway. Go through this then bear half right following a right-hand hedge then the outside edge of a wood called Widmore Plantation past a pond, through a bridlegate and on to the far end of the next field. Here take bridleway MX16, a woodland track straight on into a wood called Park Thorns. After about 30 yards turn right through a New Zealand (barbed-wire) gate and over a culvert onto path MX10 and follow this grassy track for 130 yards. Where the track forks, bear slightly right onto a track between a fenced young plantation and a mature cypress plantation. After 25 yards turn left over a rail-stile and bear half right across the young plantation crossing two further stiles to reach a small gate out of the wood. Bear half right across the corner of a field to a hedge gap by a corner of the wood, then follow the outside edge of the wood straight on through two fields to a gate onto the B4031.

Cross this road and turn left along its verge. At a crossroads cross the entrance to the Fulwell and Westbury road then bear half right over a stile onto path MX10. Follow the right-hand hedge to a second stile, then bear left across the field to another stile. Now bear half right across the next field to its far corner. Here cross a double stile and take path MX9 following the right-hand hedge straight on. Where this hedge wiggles left, go straight on over another double stile then continue beside a left-hand hedge to a stile in the corner leading to some stables. Cross this and two further stiles by white gates, then continue to a white gate onto a road on the edge of Mixbury.

Turn right onto this road following it through the village with its brick and stone estate cottages and pollarded lime trees. By the war memorial, fork right through a kissing-gate onto path MX25 into the churchyard along a macadam path passing right of the Norman church built by Roger de Ivery in about 1074 with fine Norman tracery around its doorway. On reaching a kissing-gate onto a road opposite the remains of Beaumont Castle built in about 1100 but now only earthworks, turn left. At a road junction turn right and take the road out of the village looking out for a view of Mixbury House beyond the last house to your left.

At a sharp left-hand bend, fork right onto bridleway MX22 taking a rough track across a field to the left-hand end of a row of Scots pines where you take a causeway straight on across the former Great Central railway cutting. Now take a grassy track straight on across the next field with views ahead towards Westbury and to your left towards the outskirts of the Northamptonshire town of Brackley. On reaching the far hedge turn left onto bridleway MX4 following a right-hand hedge downhill to a gate leading to a former level crossing over the Banbury-Buckingham railway (opened in 1850 and closed in 1961). Cross the old railway to reach a bridge over the Great Ouse into Buckinghamshire. Here take bridleway WB15 following a right-hand hedge straight on, then continuing across a field towards a white gate ahead. On passing through a sporadic hedge line, turn right through a gate into a factory yard by Westbury Mill and follow its access road called Mill Lane straight on to reach Westbury village by a large seventeenth-century ironstone manor house, now part of Beachborough Preparatory School.

By a thatched cottage called Little Thatches turn right onto path WB13 following a macadam drive. After 10 yards turn left and follow a left-hand fence to a second drive. Here go straight on through a squeeze-stile and along a sunken path past an ancient pillory to your right to reach a road. Turn right onto this, then at a left-hand bend take path WB10 straight on through a kissing-gate into Westbury churchyard. Now fork immediately left onto a grassy path passing left of the twelfth-century church and bearing slightly left, then

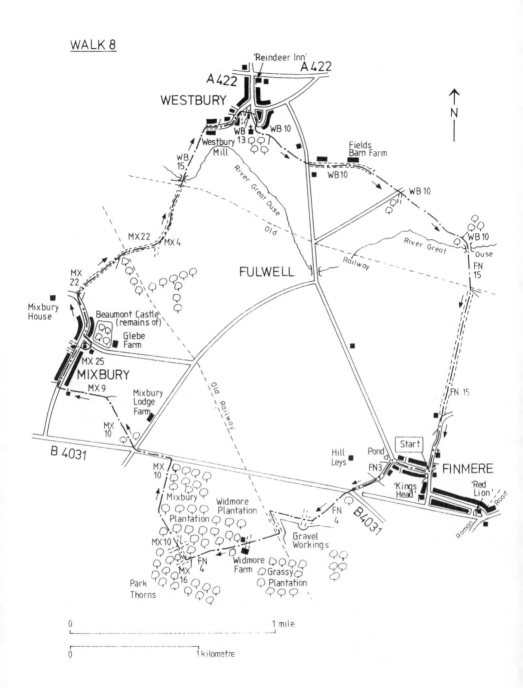

WALK 8

continuing through a gate and along the right-hand edge of a garden to a stile into a field. Keep straight on across the field towards the corner of the hedge, crossing a stile then a culvert by the corner of the hedge and following it uphill to a gate and stile onto a road. Cross this bearing half right to a gate virtually opposite. Go through this and take a macadam drive straight on. At Fields Barn Farm the road becomes concreted and then loses its surface and you follow a rough track straight on with views towards Water Stratford and Buckingham with its prominent church spire ahead, passing another farm and continuing to gates onto a road. Cross the road and go through a gate opposite, then ignoring a grassy track beside a copse, keep straight on across a field to a hedge gap. Continue across the next field to a hedge gap with a concealed ditch and sheep-wire fence. Cross the ditch and fence then bear half left to the left-hand end of a copse. Here bear right across a culvert then go straight on to a footbridge over the Great Ouse.

Cross this and now back in Oxfordshire, take path FN15 bearing slightly right over a rise passing left of an electricity pole to reach gates at an old railway crossing on the Banbury–Buckingham line. Now bear slightly right onto a grass track lined with newly-planted trees, heading for Finmere Church when this comes into view, to reach a gateway leading to a bend in a road, then follow this road straight on past the church to your starting point.

WALK 9 :   HETHE

Length of Walk:	(A) 8.0 miles / 12.9 Km
	(B) 3.9 miles / 6.3 Km
	(C) 6.3 miles / 10.2 Km
Starting Point:	Hethe War Memorial.
Grid Ref:	SP594295
Maps:	OS Landranger Sheets 152 & 164
	OS Pathfinder Sheets 1045 (SP43/53) &
	1069 (SP 42/52) (all) + 1046 (SP63/73) &
	1070 (SP62/72) (A & B only)

How to get there / Parking: Hethe, 4 miles north of Bicester, may be reached from the town by taking the A421 towards Buckingham. After 3.5 miles turn left onto a road signposted to Fringford and Hethe. In Fringford turn left and then right. After a further 0.8 miles turn left again for Hethe. At a small village green by the war memorial limited parking is possible but additional space is available further on.

Hethe, a corruption of 'heath', is an attractive village spread out along a winding street with a fourteenth-century clerestoried church restored by the noted architect George Street in 1859. In the twelfth century one of the village farms was given by the court jester Rahere to St. Bartholomew's Priory, London, which he had built, as a source of revenue for its upkeep and this connection survived for over 800 years before the farm was finally sold.

All three walks explore the country to the north of Hethe with its mixture of parkland, woodland and arable, which came to literary prominence in the 1940s with the publication of Flora Thompson's 'Lark Rise to Candleford' vividly depicting Oxfordshire village life in the 1880s and 1890s. Walks A and B first lead you towards Fringford (or Candleford Green in Flora Thompson's book) before turning north to the lost village of Willaston and the beauties of Shelswell Park and continuing to Cottisford (or Fordlow) where Flora Thompson and her heroine Laura went to school. Walk B then returns to Hethe while Walk C leads you direct to Cottisford before joining Walk A and continuing to Juniper Hill (or Lark Rise) where

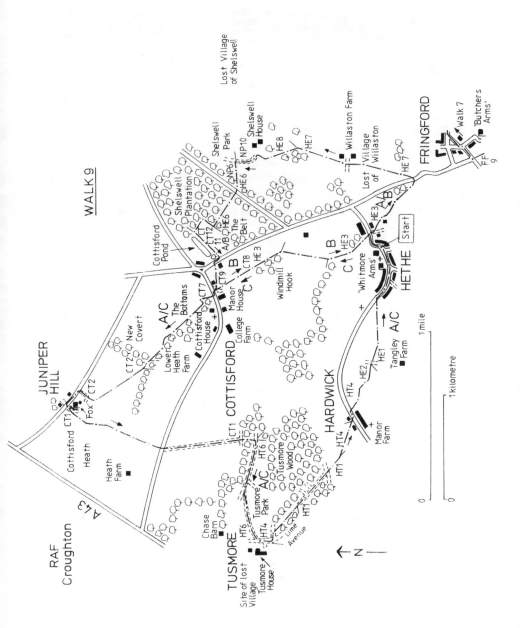

WALK 9

RAF Croughton

A43

JUNIPER HILL

Cottisford CT1
Heath
Fox CT2
CT2

Heath Farm

New Covert
A/C
CT2
The Bottoms
Lower
Heath Farm
Cottisford
House
CT7

Cottisford Pond

Cottisford Plantation
Shelswell
CT12
CT11
A/B HE6
The Belt
HE6
NP6
NP10
Shelswell Park
Shelswell House
HE8
HE7

Lost Village of Shelswell

Willaston Farm
HE7
Lost Village of Willaston
HE7

FRINGFORD
walk 7
'Butchers Arms'
FP
9

Manor House
College Farm
CT8
C
B
CT9
HE3
HE3
A/B
B
C
HE3
'Whitmore Arms'

Windmill Hook

HE THE
Start
A/C
HE1
HE2
Tangley Farm

HARDWICK
HT4
HT4
HT4
HT1
Manor Farm

COTTISFORD
CT1

Tusmore Wood
HT6
A/C
Tusmore Park
HT4

TUSMORE
Site of lost Village
Tusmore House
HT6
HT4
Lime Avenue
HT1

Chase Barn

N

1 mile
1 kilometre
0
0

54

Flora (and Laura) were born. From here Walks A and C return by way of Cottisford Heath, more beautiful parkland at Tusmore and the tiny village of Hardwick to reach Hethe.

Walks A, B and C start from the war memorial in Hethe and take the Fringford road for 200 yards. After crossing a bridge, **Walk C** turns left over a stile onto path HE3. Not omit the next three paragraphs.

Walks A and B turn right onto path HE3, a rough lane. Where the lane bears right by a weeping willow, leave it and go straight on uphill to a corner of the sewage works hedge then follow a right-hand hedge straight on. Where this hedge ends, cross a stile and follow a left-hand fence straight on, passing a copse to reach a gate and stile onto the Fringford road. Now take path HE7 through gates opposite bearing half left uphill to cross a stile then follow a right-hand hedge through a plantation and a field to the bottom of a dip. Here start to diverge from the hedge and cross the site of the lost village of Willaston, of which only earthworks remain, and the drive to Willaston Farm to reach the right-hand of two gates in the fence ahead. Now keep straight on, heading just right of a large oak tree at the right-hand end of a copse ahead and continuing to a stile into Shelswell Park in the bottom of a dip. Here take path HE8 bearing slightly left to go between a scots pine and two large sycamores then cross a stile left of a kink in a wooden fence and bear half right across the next parkland field heading for a very tall lime tree, with views of the ruins of Shelswell Park house to your right. On nearing this tree, bear right to cross a stile by gates then take path NP10, a stone-based track, straight on gradually swinging right to join a right-hand fence. By a bridlegate in this fence turn left off the track onto bridleway NP6 (later HE6) crossing the parkland and passing just right of a large beech tree to reach a bridlegate onto a road.

Cross this road and take bridleway HE6 straight on beside a right-hand fence to a bridlegate into a field then along the edge of a tree belt to the far side of the field. Here go straight on through a tree belt into the next field then turn right onto path CT12 beside the edge of Shelswell Plantation around two sides of the field to a gate and stile. Now turn left onto path CT11 along the shore of an attractive lake called Cottisford Pond then the edge of a copse to a gate and stile onto a road. Turn right onto this road. Just past Kennel Cottages turn left onto their drive then immediately right over a stile onto path CT9 following a left-hand fence past the cottages. Where the fence turns left, bear half right across the field crossing a fence and continuing to a small gate between a tennis court and an electricity sub-station. Now turn right through a hedge gap and left onto a drive. Just before the drive turns left, **Walk A** turns right through a small gate onto path CT8 rejoining Walk C. Now omit the next two paragraphs.

At the same point **Walk B** turns left onto path CT8 crossing a lawn and passing left of some bushes to a small gate. Now follow a right-hand fence downhill through two paddocks to a stile over two fences then bear slightly right across wasteland to a concealed hedge gap leading to a footbridge and stile. Here bear slightly left across a field heading just left of a tall ash tree on the skyline to go through a hedge gap left of double gates. Now take path HE3 beside a right-hand hedge generally straight on through two fields. Near the far end of the second field go straight on over a rail stile in a wiggle in the hedge and continue between the hedge and a stream to a stile onto the road at Hethe then turn right onto the road for your starting point.

Walk C takes path HE3 straight on between a stream and a hedge, keeping left of a wiggle in the hedge then following it to cross a rail stile. Now follow a left-hand hedge straight on through two fields. At the far end of the second field go through a hedge gap and take path CT8 straight on towards a twin-poled electricity pylon to cross a stile and footbridge. Here bear slightly right through wasteland to cross a concealed stile over two fences then follow a left-hand fence uphill over two stiles into a paddock. Now bear left passing through a gate and right of some bushes to cross a drive and continue through a gate rejoining **Walk A**.

Walks A and C now take a drive straight on to the village street in Cottisford, the mother village of Fordlow in 'Lark Rise to Candleford' which, with its heavily restored thirteenth-century church, remains much as Flora Thompson describes it. Turn left onto this road then opposite the drive to Duffus House turn right through a gap onto path CT7 alongside a tree belt. Where the tree belt turns left, do likewise soon turning right and following the edge of a wood until it gives way to a hedge. Here turn left through a hedge gap and continue along the edge of the wood to the next field corner. Ignoring a branching path to your left, go straight on through a wood called New Covert to enter another field. Here fork half right onto path CT2 crossing the field diagonally, with views of RAF Croughton to your left, to cross a stile left of the corner of a hedge. Now take a fenced path, later a grassy track straight on to a road at Juniper Hill.

Juniper Hill (or Lark Rise) is a relatively recent settlement first established on Cottisford Heath by the parish in 1754 to house the parish poor. Originally accessible only by footpath, a road was built when Cottisford Heath was enclosed in 1854 but as Flora Thompson's book testifies, it remained poor in the 1880s and 1890s.

Turn left onto this road and follow it through the hamlet past the 'Fox'. Opposite Larkwell Nurseries turn left onto path CT1, a rough lane. Where the lane bears left, leave it going straight on through a hedge gap and following a left-hand hedge straight on through two fields to the Cottisford road. Cross this and a stile by gates opposite into a green lane. On emerging into a field, fork left onto a grassy track beside a left-hand hedge and follow it to the edge of a wood. Go straight on over a footbridge into the wood then pass right of a corner of a fenced enclosure and follow the fence to the second gate in it. Now turn right onto bridleway HT6, a grassy track into Tusmore Park along the edge of the wood with glimpses of Tusmore House ahead. On reaching a fork by a gate, go straight on through the gate and follow a grassy track straight on across open parkland. At a further fork keep left heading initially for a cottage ahead then gradually bearing left towards Tusmore House to reach gates onto a macadam drive.

Tusmore House, near the site of the lost village of Tusmore which disappeared in the fourteenth century after its population was wiped out by the Black Death, is the latest of a series of houses on this site being built as recently as 1965. The previous house built by the Roman Catholic Fermor family in the 1760s was destroyed by fire in 1840 and rebuilt by the Earl of Effingham in 1857 before being demolished in 1960, while its predecessor, also built by the Fermors when they moved there from Somerton in 1642, was visited by the poet Alexander Pope whose 'The Rape of the Lock' was based on Arabella Fermor.

Turn left onto this drive (bridleway HT4) passing the ornamental gates to the house. Go through gates on the drive then turn left off it through a gate onto a grassy track. After a few yards bear half right off the track to follow an avenue of lime trees for a quarter mile to gates into Tusmore Wood. Now take bridleway HT1 straight on through the gates and along an avenue of yew trees. At the far side of the wood ignore a crossing track and go straight on across a field towards the red-tiled roof of Manor Farm at Hardwick. Midway between a pair of oaks and a single oak to your left, fork half left onto path HT4 heading for the gable end of a grey council house, with Hardwick's tiny mediaeval church restored after 1857 by the Earl of Effingham visible in places to your right, to reach a gap in a stone wall at the back of some gardens. Here bear half right onto a fenced path to Hardwick village street onto which you turn left.

Just past the last right-hand cottage turn right through a gate onto path HT4 bearing half left across a field to its far corner. Here cross a fence and bear slightly left across a field to an electricity pole at the left-hand end of a hedge. Now bear slightly right across the next field to a corner where you turn right through a hedge gap then left onto path HE2 following the hedge to a field corner. Here take bridleway HE1 straight on through a hedge gap and across a field to a tall oak tree then follow a right-hand hedge straight on for a quarter mile to Hardwick Road on the edge of Hethe with views to your right towards Brill Hill and the distant Chilterns. Turn right onto this road and take it straight on through the village for a third of a mile to your starting point.

Length of Walk:	(A)	8.4 miles / 13.6 Km
	(B)	6.4 miles / 10.3 Km
	(C)	3.4 miles / 5.5 Km
Starting Point:		Road junction near the 'Fox', Souldern.
Grid Ref:		SP521315
Maps:		OS Landranger Sheets 151 (all) &
		164 (A/B only)
		OS Pathfinder Sheets 1045 (SP43/53) (all)
		& 1069 (SP 42/52) (A/B only)

How to get there / Parking: Souldern, 7 miles northwest of Bicester, may be reached from the town by taking the B4100 towards Aynho. After 6.5 miles, just past the 'Bear Inn', turn left onto the road into Souldern. Go past the village pond to your right, then keep straight on and where the village street widens out, find a suitable parking place.

Notes: Flooding is possible in places after heavy rain.

Souldern, on the slopes of Ploughley Hill, meeting place of the ancient Ploughley Hundred above the Cherwell valley, is believed by some historians to date only from the twelfth century when the building of its present church commenced and the first known written reference to it was made, while others consider that, despite its not being mentioned in the Domesday Book, a pagan Saxon burial discovered nearby suggests much earlier habitation. Today the village with its fine Cotswold-stone houses gives the impression of past affluence and this may explain why it captivated the poet William Wordsworth on a visit to his friend Robert Jones, the contemporary rector, to the extent that he made it the subject of a sonnet entitled 'A Parsonage in Oxfordshire'.

Walks A and B start by taking you along the hillside above the Cherwell valley with its fine views to the ancient riverside village of Somerton before following the Oxford Canal Towpath to Souldern Wharf and climbing a low hill with panoramic views, while Walks A and C lead you with more fine views to the hilltop Northamptonshire village of Aynho with its imposing manor house.

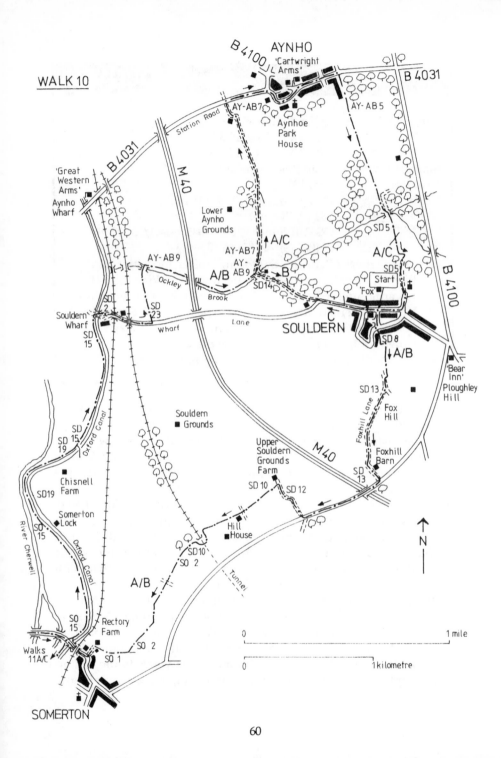

WALK 10

60

Walks A and B start from the road junction near the 'Fox' in Souldern and follow a narrow lane called Fox Lane past this inn to a T-junction. Here turn right then immediately left over a slippery green stile onto fenced path SD8. Ignore a branching path to your left then by a small pond turn left to cross another slippery green stile. Now bear slightly right across a field to join a right-hand hedge at the top of Fox Hill level with a line of oak trees. Here turn right over a stone stile into a green lane called Foxhill Lane (bridleway SD13) then turn left into it passing some gates to your right. Where the lane forks, go right and follow a fenced bridleway with fine views in places through gaps in the right-hand hedge across the Cherwell valley. Eventually you enter a sunken green lane, pass Foxhill Barn and climb to reach a road.

Turn right onto this road and follow it over the M40 with wide views across the Cherwell valley to your right. After nearly half a mile turn right onto bridleway SD12, the macadam drive to Upper Souldern Grounds Farm and follow it downhill with views of Aynhoe Park House on a hilltop ahead and Souldern over Fox Hill to your right. On nearing the farm where the surface changes to concrete, turn left onto path SD10 across a field to cross a footbridge and a rail stile by a sycamore tree. Now go straight on towards the right-hand end of a barn ahead with a fine view to your right of the magnificent brick railway viaduct on the Banbury–Marylebone line opened in 1910. Near the barn cross a concrete road then bear slightly right across a field passing Hill House to your left and aiming for the middle of a copse ahead concealing the mouth of a railway tunnel to cross a stile. Here turn left and follow a fenced path around the mouth of the tunnel to cross a stile leading you into a coniferous plantation then turn left through the plantation until you emerge into a field.

Take path SO2 straight on across the field, with fine views towards North Aston Church and Hall ahead, to go through a hedge gap and descend some steps just left of the far corner. Here cross a green lane then go through a hedge gap opposite into another field. Go straight on across this over a ridge to pass through a gap in the right-hand hedge by an ash tree with Somerton and North Aston coming into view ahead. Now turn left and follow the left-hand hedge. On nearing the bottom of a dip, bear half right across the field heading right of a modern barn ahead, with views towards Deddington to your right, to reach a gate by the far end of the right-hand hedge. Do NOT go through this gate but turn right through a hedge gap onto path SO1 following a left-hand hedge and fence downhill to reach a stile. Cross this and continue downhill crossing a second stile and taking a fenced path to cross a third, then turn left onto the gravel drive to Rectory Farm to reach a road at Somerton.

Somerton, on a hillside above the Cherwell valley, is first recorded in the eighth century when Ethelbald of Mercia captured it from Wessex. Four hundred years later it was the site of a castle, but all trace of this has vanished, and the church was built which contains a number of interesting tombs of the Fermor family who lived at the former manor house but moved to Tusmore Park in the seventeenth century. In the same century, William Juxon, a former rector of Somerton, was made Archbishop of Canterbury at the Restoration.

Turn right onto this road and follow it under a railway bridge and over the Oxford Canal to meet the route of **Walk 11** then turn right onto a fenced path leading to the canal bank. Here turn left onto the towpath (SO15) and follow it for 1.7 miles, passing Somerton Lock, then as SD19 (later SD15) passing close to the railway viaduct seen earlier and a swingbridge to reach Souldern Wharf. Here at brick-built bridge no.192 leave the towpath and cross a stile then turn right onto bridleway SD2 crossing the bridge and joining a road called Wharf Lane. Take this straight on over one railway bridge then under a second. Having rounded a left-hand bend, just past the first left-hand electricity pole turn left through a hedge gap onto path SD23 following a left-hand fence with panoramic views in all directions with North Aston and Clifton to your left, Adderbury church spire ahead, Aynho church to your right and Hill House and Somerton behind, as well as fine railway viaducts both ahead and behind. Keep straight on downhill to a bridge over a stream, now with a close view of the viaduct to your left, then bear slightly right to cross a bridge over Ockley Brook marking the Northamptonshire boundary. Here turn right onto path AY–AB9 following the brook to pass under the M40 then bear slightly left to reach a farm road, onto which you turn right. On approaching a bridge over the brook, turn left through gates into a field and follow the brook for a further third of a mile to cross a stile and reach a gate through which **Walk A** goes straight on joining **Walk C**. Now omit the next two paragraphs.

Walk B turns right here over a stile and footbridge onto bridleway SD14, a green lane with concrete wheel-tracks, by Souldern Mill with its attractive garden, then follows this lane uphill for a third of a mile to rejoin Wharf Lane, onto which you turn left to enter Souldern and reach your starting point.

Walk C starts at the road junction near the 'Fox' and takes the main village street westwards out of the village. At a sharp left-hand bend leave the road and take bridleway SD14, a green lane with concrete wheel tracks, straight on downhill for a third of a mile, eventually passing Souldern Mill with its attractive garden and crossing a bridge then a culvert over Ockley Brook to enter Northamptonshire where you bear right.

Walks A and C now take bridleway AY–AB7, a grassy track with concrete wheel tracks, straight on uphill for over a third of a mile, eventually joining the Aynho Park wall where there is a fine view of Aynhoe Park House and Aynho Church ahead. For some reason, the name of the house has traditionally always been spelt with an 'e' while the village and all other names are spelt without! Seat of the Cartwright family from 1615 to 1960, Aynhoe Park House was set on fire by the Royalists in 1645 while retreating to Oxford after the Battle of Naseby. The present house with its two fronts, one facing the park and one facing the village street, dates from the seventeenth century but was altered and extended by Sir John Soane in 1800–5. The church was rebuilt by Edward Wing in about 1725 but retains the fourteenth-century tower of the mediaeval church and contains numerous monuments to the Cartwright family.

Here bear slightly left to join a macadam farm road. Take it straight on for half a mile to reach the B4031 where there is a fine view ahead towards Adderbury and King's Sutton. Turn right onto its rough footway and follow it uphill into the Cotswold-stone village of Aynho, known as 'the apricot village' because a mediaeval lord of the manor took part of the rents in apricots which are still grown in Aynho today. At a T-junction cross the B4100, then turn right onto its pavement and follow it round a left-hand bend past Aynhoe Park House, the church, the 'Cartwright Arms Hotel' and Grammar House, a former school built in 1617. Where the left-hand pavement ends, cross the B4100 and continue along its right-hand pavement to its junction with Portway.

Here turn right over a broken stone stile onto walled path AY–AB5. Follow it for some 350 yards, at one point passing through a tunnel before emerging over a stile into Aynho Park with fine views towards

Souldern ahead and across the Cherwell valley to your right. Now follow a right-hand fence straight on downhill past some woodland and through a set of gates, then go straight on across a field to the corner of a fence and continue beside it downhill to cross a stile in it. Here take a track straight on into a wood crossing a bridge over Ockley Brook into Oxfordshire then taking path SD5 straight on to cross a stile by a gate. Now follow a right-hand fence straight on over a rise ignoring two stiles in it. By the corner of a tree belt concealing a sewage works turn left to reach a third stile. Cross this and take a path between the sewage works fence and a stream to the works entrance, then turn left onto its drive and follow it to the end of a road by Souldern Church. Take this road straight on to a T-junction by the village pond then turn right for your starting point.

WALK 11: UPPER HEYFORD

Length of Walk:	(A) 8.8 miles / 14.2 Km
	(B) 5.8 miles / 9.3 Km
	(C) 4.7 miles / 7.5 Km
Starting Point:	(A/B) Upper Heyford Church.
	(C) Telephone box at North Aston Green.
Grid Ref:	(A/B) SP495259 / (C) SP478290
Maps:	OS Landranger Sheet 164
	OS Pathfinder Sheet 1069 (SP42/52)

How to get there / Parking: (A/B) Upper Heyford, 6 miles west of Bicester, may be reached from the town by taking the A4095 towards Witney. Where the A4095 turns left, take the B4030 straight on towards Enstone. Nearly a mile beyond its junction with the B430 at Middleton Stoney at a sharp left-hand bend, fork right onto the Upper Heyford road and follow it straight on for over 2 miles past the airbase to a T-junction in the village. Here turn right then take the second turning left (High Street). At a T-junction turn left into Church Walk and park by the church.

(C) North Aston, 8 miles northwest of Bicester, may be reached by leaving the M40 at Junction 10 (Ardley) and taking the B430 towards Middleton Stoney. After half a mile turn right onto a road signposted to Somerton. At a T-junction in Somerton, turn right and continue for 1.5 miles to North Aston where you can park by the right-hand green.

Notes: These walks should not be attempted when the River Cherwell is in flood.

Upper Heyford is today best known for its US airbase which was used for bombing Libya and where cruise missiles were stationed in the 1980s in the face of vociferous protest. First established as a British base during the First World War, Upper Heyford gradually expanded and was used by Bomber Command in the Second World War before being taken over by the Americans in 1951. It has now closed down and its future use is currently the subject of controversial debate. In contrast, the village, set on the eastern

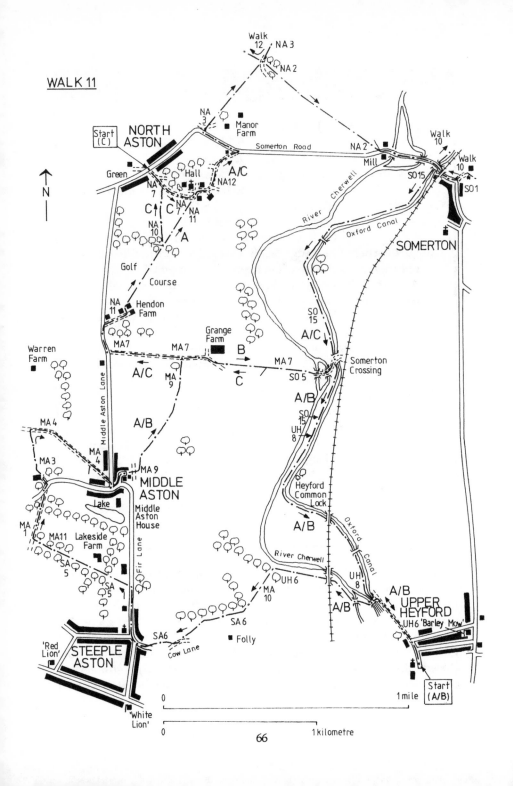

WALK 11

slopes of the Cherwell valley is now a quiet place with idyllic views across the valley.

All three walks explore this beautiful section of the Cherwell valley with a whole series of glorious views which can now be enjoyed without the noise disturbance which plagued the area for so many years. Each walk includes a section of the Oxford Canal towpath and visits at least one of the attractive, yet very varied trio of Astons on the western slopes of the valley.

Walks A and B start by Upper Heyford Church, which, apart from its fifteenth-century tower, was rebuilt in Victorian times, and take Church Walk northwards with fine views to your left across the Cherwell valley towards Steeple Aston. At two road junctions keep straight on, entering Allens Lane. At a sharp left-hand bend, take path UH6 straight on over a stile by a gate and along a stony track to a bridge over the Oxford Canal, built by James Brindley in the 1780s to link the Thames to the industrial Midlands. Turn left over this and a second bridge over an arm of the Cherwell, then bear half right across a meadow, later with views to your left towards Lower Heyford, to cross a bridge over another arm of the river. Here turn right and follow the riverbank to a bridge under the Oxford–Banbury railway. At the far end, a view opens out towards Middle Aston ahead and North Aston to your right. Go straight on across a meadow to rejoin the riverbank at a bend in the river, then follow it looking out for the handrail of a footbridge to your left.

Now turn left across the meadow and footbridge and take path MA10 straight on through a belt of trees and uphill across a field to go through a small gate at the left-hand end of a copse where a folly built by the landscape gardener William Kent in 1738 to terminate the view from Rousham Park comes into view ahead. Turn right onto path SA6 following a right-hand tree belt uphill. At the top of the hill, views open out towards Steeple Aston ahead, Rousham Park, built for Sir Robert Dormer in 1635 and extended by William Kent in the 1730s, to your left and Upper Heyford over your left shoulder. Where the hedge bears slightly right, bear slightly left across the corner of the field to a small green gate into Cow Lane. Turn right into this lane then fork immediately right over a rail stile by a green gate and cross a further stile in the bushes ahead. Now follow a right-hand hedge uphill through two paddocks to a gate and stile leading to a village street in the mainly ironstone village of Steeple Aston.

Go straight on up this street. At a T-junction turn right to reach a second junction by the thirteenth-century church, which contains a large monument by Scheemaker to the eighteenth-century 'hanging judge', Sir Francis Page of Middle Aston and his wife. This nickname resulted from the fact that during his career he sentenced more than 100 criminals to death! Here take Fir Lane straight on out of the village, then at a slight left-hand bend turn left through a kissing-gate onto enclosed path SA5. Follow this straight on for a third of a mile, soon entering a belt of trees and later ignoring a gap into a right-hand field and taking path MA11 straight on through a further tree belt until you emerge onto a track (MA1). Turn right onto this track following a right-hand hedge then passing through a copse to reach a road on the edge of Middle Aston where there is a large ornamental lake to your right.

Turn right onto this road then immediately left onto path MA3 along a concrete drive to cross a stile by a gate. Here bear right past a small factory, then cross a stile by an old gate and bear half left across a field to cross a stile in the top hedge. Bear slightly left across the next field heading just left of Warren Farm and a radio mast to reach bridleway MA4, a crossing grassy track. Turn right onto this, soon with a hedge to your left. On leaving the hedge behind, go straight across a field with fine views across the Cherwell valley towards Upper Heyford ahead and Somerton to your left joining a right-hand fence, where you ignore a stile to your right, then a gravel drive and continuing to a road in Middle Aston.

Turn right onto this, then at a T-junction turn left. At a right-hand bend turn left again onto a rough road towards a stone building with a clocktower, then bear right past some cottages. Where the road ends, take path MA9 straight on through a gate, then pass left of a double garage to a stile at the rear corner of the garden. Go straight on through a small orchard, across a drive and wooden rails opposite and past the end of a hedge, then turn left and follow the hedge to a corner of the field. Here cross a footbridge right of a willow tree and bear half right across a field towards Grange Farm, with a view of North Aston Hall ahead, to cross a culvert by the left-hand end of a hedge. Now go straight on across the next field joining the right-hand hedge by an oak tree. Where the hedge bears left, go straight on through it and a small plantation to reach bridleway MA7, a macadam farm road, onto which **Walk A** turns left joining **Walk C**. Now omit the next paragraph.

Walk B turns right onto it and follows it to Grange Farm. Here bear slightly right onto a grassy track towards a gate then ignore this gate and go through a second. Now leave the track and go straight on across the field to a white bridlegate. Go through this and take a hedged bridleway straight on to another gate. Now keep straight on over a bridge and culvert to cross a gated bridge over the River Cherwell. Here take bridleway SO5, a green lane, straight on ignoring a branching track to your left, crossing another bridge and reaching a gate. Go through this then turn right through a second gate to reach the Oxford Canal towpath (SO15) onto which you turn right rejoining **Walk A**. Now omit the next five paragraphs.

Walks A and C now follow bridleway MA7 uphill for a third of a mile to reach Middle Aston Lane. Turn right onto this road with fine views across the Cherwell valley to your right. Just before a cottage turn right through a gate onto path NA11, the macadam drive to Hendon Farm and follow it to the farm. Here turn left over a stile left of an old stable-block, then by the back of the building bear slightly right across a paddock to a stile by a small stone building where a fine view opens out across the valley towards Somerton. Bear half right downhill across a golf course to the right-hand end of a reed-filled pond, then go straight on uphill to the central of three gaps in the top hedge where North Aston Hall and Church come into view ahead. Here **Walk A** keeps straight on towards the church, crossing two fences (if still obstructed, follow Walk C) and passing left of an oak tree to a hedge gap in the field corner where you join a gravel drive and follow it straight on to a fork by a lychgate. Now omit the next paragraph. **Walk C** bears slightly left onto path NA10 soon crossing a stile and following a left-hand hedge. On reaching the gravel drive to the church (path NA7), bear left onto it and retrace your steps to North Aston Green.

Walk C starts from the telephone box at the southeast corner of North Aston Green opposite an old stone fountain, crosses the road and takes path NA7, the gravel drive to St. Mary's Church ignoring a branching macadam drive to your left and with a fine view opening out ahead across the Cherwell valley towards the Heyfords, then with a view to your left of the seventeenth-century North Aston Hall, which incongruously dwarfs the fourteenth-century church with a fifteenth-century tower, less than two feet away.

At a fork by a lychgate, **Walks A and C** turn right onto path NA12, another gravel drive, ignoring a branching drive to your left. At a further fork by a cottage go straight on with fine views opening out to your right across the Cherwell valley towards Somerton. Disregard a branching drive to The Manor to your left and bear right to reach lodge gates onto Somerton Road. Turn left onto this road and follow it uphill. At a left-hand bend turn right onto path NA3, a macadam farm drive, then at a junction of drives go straight on through double gates into a field with a view towards Deddington to your left. Here bear half right over the top of a hill passing just right of an electricity pole and continuing with fine views ahead towards a brick viaduct on the Marylebone–Banbury railway and the Northamptonshire village of Aynho, to reach the left-hand set of double gates in the far corner of the field. Go through these to meet the route of **Walk 12** and turn right and follow a right-hand fence. After about 25 yards turn right over a stile onto path NA2 bearing slightly left across a plantation to a stile at the far side where Somerton comes into view ahead. Now head for the left-hand end of Somerton village to reach double gates and rails left of an oak tree in the bottom of the dip. Cross the rails and head for a tall lime tree left of Somerton's twelfth-century church to reach a gate onto Somerton Road.

Turn left onto this road rounding a blind bend then passing a former mill and crossing bridges over the millstream, a pond and the main River Cherwell. On approaching the Oxford Canal bridge by a village nameboard (where you briefly meet the route of **Walk 10**), turn right through a gap in a stone wall onto the canal towpath (SO15). Follow this straight on for a mile with views to your right towards North Aston and Middle Aston in places, passing the remains of a swingbridge, going through a gate, under a bridge and later through two more gates. On approaching bridge no.199, **Walk A** goes straight on through a gate, under the bridge and through another gate to rejoin **Walk B**. Now omit the next paragraph.

Walk C does NOT go under bridge no.199 but bears right to pass through a green gate into a green lane (bridleway SO5), then turns right onto it passing through a second green gate, ignoring a branching track to the right and crossing a bridge over the main arm of the Cherwell. Now take bridleway MA7 straight on through a gate, across a culvert and a small bridge and through a gate into a narrow green lane. On emerging through a bridlegate at the far end into a field, go straight on to a gate left of Grange Farm, then follow a grassy track straight on to join a macadam farm drive. Bear slightly left onto this, soon rejoining **Walk A**. Now go back five paragraphs.

Walks A and B now follow the canal towpath (SO15, later UH8) straight on for over a mile passing Middle Aston to your right and Heyford Common Lock, then going under a railway bridge and two brick arches. After passing under the second, turn right up the bank to cross a rail stile, then turn right onto path UH6 crossing the bridge, passing through a gate and turning right onto a stone track. Now retrace your steps into Upper Heyford.

WALK 12: DEDDINGTON

Length of Walk: 5.9 miles / 9.5 Km
Starting Point: Southeast corner of Deddington Market Place.
Grid Ref: SP467316
Maps: OS Landranger Sheets 151 & 164
OS Pathfinder Sheets 1045 (SP43/53)
& 1069 (SP42/52)
How to get there / Parking: Deddington, 5.5 miles south of
Banbury, may be reached from the town by taking the A4260.
At the traffic lights in Deddington turn left onto the B4031 to
reach the Market Place where there is ample parking.
Notes: In 1996 path DD8 was obstructed in two places.
If you have to deviate from the official line described,
take care not to damage fences or trample crops.

Deddington, on a hilltop above the Swere and Cherwell valleys, can be identified for miles around by its massive square pinnacled church tower. This tower, which had to be rebuilt in the seventeenth century after the collapse of its predecessor in 1635, symbolises the wealth and importance the little town once enjoyed. Located at the crossroads of two former major roads, the A4260 from Oxford to Banbury and the B4031 from Buckingham to Chipping Norton, Deddington was of strategic importance and so became the site of a twelfth-century castle where the Earl of Warwick imprisoned the royal favourite, Piers Gaveston, prior to his execution at Blacklow Hill in 1312. The massive grass ramparts, which are all that now remain of the castle, can be seen on the edge of the village. The fourteenth-century church, as its tower would suggest, is also of sizeable proportions and the Market Place which it dominates, is both spacious and surrounded by fine ironstone houses. Deddington's decline in importance may perhaps be explained by the fact that its hilltop location led to first the Oxford Canal and then the railways passing it by in favour of Banbury and so while Banbury prospered and grew, Deddington became virtually fossilised in its eighteenth-century form.

The walk, however, takes advantage of its location by first taking your northeastwards towards the confluence of the Cherwell and the Swere with wide views across these valleys before turning south to the riverside hamlet of Clifton. You then continue southwards with more fine views of the Cherwell valley before circling back to Deddington.

Starting from the southeast corner of Deddington Market Place, take the B4031 towards Buckingham and follow its winding course for a third of a mile ignoring side turnings and passing the path to the site of Deddington Castle. Near the edge of the village at the junction with Earl's Lane, cross the entrance to this side road and a stile onto path DD2, then cross a field to the corner of a garden hedge. Here bear slightly left passing left of a clump of trees to cross a footbridge in the back hedge of the field. Now bear slightly right across another field to a gate and rails in the far corner leading to a concrete farm road. Turn left onto this road and follow it with a fine view across the Cherwell valley towards the Northamptonshire village of Aynho on a hilltop to your right. On nearing a farm called Field Barn, Adderbury's mediaeval church spire then comes into view to your left. At the farm continue to follow the concrete road (now on path DD3) passing right of the farmhouse. Where the road forks, go straight on, soon bearing slightly right onto a stone farm road leading out of the farm where fine views open out to your left and ahead across the Swere and Cherwell valleys with Adderbury spire to the north, King's Sutton spire to the northeast and Aynho on a hilltop ahead. At a T-junction of farm roads turn left soon passing through some gates. Here turn left off the road following a left-hand fence, later a hedge. Where the hedge wiggles to the right, leave it and bear half right across the field aiming for two trees in its bottom corner. Here turn right onto bridleway DD4, a farm road known as Tithe Lane, and follow it straight on for nearly a mile eventually reaching a residential road in the riverside hamlet of Clifton, which borders the southwestern tip of Northamptonshire. Now follow this road straight on to the B4031.

Turn left onto its pavement passing the disused village church. By the 'Duke of Cumberland's Head' turn right into Chapel Close. Ignore Walnut Close to your left, then where Chapel Close forks, take the left-hand option, bridleway DD6, which soon becomes enclosed between a wall and a hedge. Follow this bridleway, which for about

73

half a mile is a pleasant hedged green lane with wildflowers and fine views in places across the Cherwell valley towards the brick railway viaducts on the Marylebone–Banbury railway and Somerton and later follows a left-hand fence across a field, to an old gateway at its far end. Now bear half left across the corner of the next field to join the left-hand hedge by an oak tree then follow this hedge through two fields to a bridlegate leading to the bank of a stream. Here turn left soon crossing Bowman's Bridge then take bridleway NA1 straight on along a green lane with a willow copse to your left, soon turning right to reach a gate into a field. Take path NA3 straight on uphill across the field towards a gate in its top corner with views of Somerton to your left and towards Deddington to your right.

Some 30 yards short of the gate, by a stile in the left-hand fence, where you briefly meet the route of **Walk 11**, turn right onto path NA2 heading left of Coldharbour Farm ahead, eventually reaching gates in the far corner of the field. Here turn right onto a macadam farm road and follow it uphill towards Coldharbour Farm. At the top of the hill, just before a cattle grid, turn left through gates into a field then turn right and follow a right-hand fence. Where the fence turns away right, bear slightly left across the field to a gate and footbridge in the far corner of the field. Cross this bridge, then take path DD8 following a left-hand hedge. Where the hedge turns left, bear half right across the field to an old gate just left of the corner of a hedge. Climb over this gate then turn left and follow the hedge past a barn to a gate onto the A4260. Turn right onto its footway and follow it uphill into Deddington, then turn right into St. Thomas Street. Where this road forks, keep left and continue straight on to reach the Market Place.

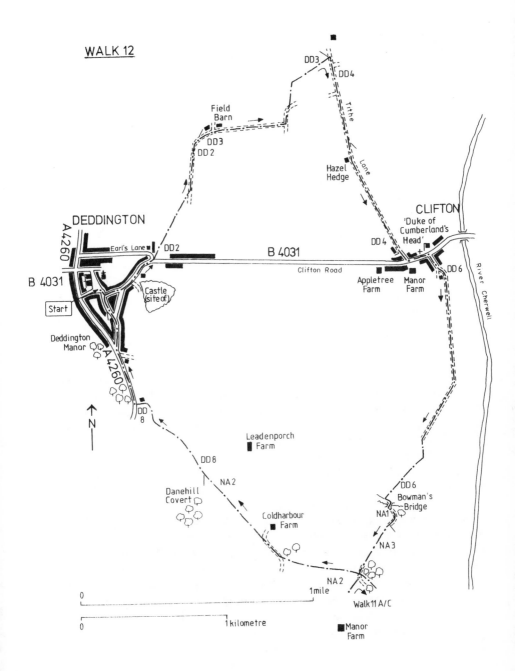

WALK 12

WALK 13 :   BARFORD ST. MICHAEL

Length of Walk: 6.5 miles / 10.5 Km
Starting Point: Junction of High Street and Townsend,
Barford St. Michael.
Grid Ref: SP436324
Maps: OS Landranger Sheets 151 & 164
OS Pathfinder Sheets 1045 (SP43/53)
& 1069 (SP42/52)

How to get there / Parking: Barford St. Michael, 5 miles south of
Banbury, may be reached from the town by taking the A361
towards Chipping Norton for 3.3 miles. At Bloxham turn left
onto a road signposted inter alia to 'The Barfords'. On
reaching Barford St. Michael, go straight on up to the top of
the hill, then turn right into Townsend (signposted to South
Newington) and look for a suitable parking place here or in
other wider village streets.

The twin villages of Barford St. Michael and Barford St. John face
each other across the Swere valley and are overlooked by RAF
Barford St. John on the hilltop to the north. Barford St. Michael,
though somewhat swamped by modern 'in-filling' development,
can boast some fine ironstone cottages with pretty gardens and a
twelfth-century church with some of the best Norman carving in the
county. In 1549 the village briefly came to national attention when
its vicar, James Webbe, led a revolt against the government's
insistence on the use of the English prayer book.

The walk explores the remote hill country to the south of the
Swere valley circling Hempton to cross the ironstone ridge west of
Deddington and then heading south to visit the tiny isolated
villages of Over and Nether Worton. The return route takes you past
Ilbury Hill with its Iron Age hill fort before crossing Steepness Hill
to return to Barford St. Michael. Though somewhat rough-going in
places, the walk compensates you with its fine views and
fascinating landscape.

Starting from the junction of High Street and Townsend in Barford St. Michael, take High Street northwards towards Banbury. After 150 yards turn right into a narrow lane called Horn Hill and follow it past some picturesque ironstone cottages. At the end of the road take path BA1 straight on between walls to a rail-stile. Here bear slightly right across a small field to a rail-stile right of a shed in the far corner, then bear slightly right across the next field joining a right-hand hedge and following it to a concealed rail-stile in a corner of the field. Now go straight on across the next field to pass through a hedge gap and follow a left-hand hedge. Where the hedge turns left, keep straight on across the field, with a view of RAF Barford St. John on the hill to your left, to cross some low rails and a sleeper footbridge in the far hedge, then continue across the next field, with a view of Hempton on the hill to your right, to reach the central of three hedge gaps ahead. Here cross a culvert then bear half right across a field to duck under a wooden rail by a small sycamore left of a larger ash tree. Now take path DD15 bearing half left across the next field to a hedge gap by a single small ash tree right of a group of small ash trees leading to Snakehill Lane.

Cross this green lane and go through a hedge gap opposite then bear slightly right across a field over the brow of the hill, with wide views opening out across the Swere valley, to a gap in the right-hand hedge 100 yards short of the far end of the field. Now bear slightly left across the next field, heading towards a large tree between telegraph poles on the skyline, to reach a concealed hunting gate. Go through this then bear half right aiming just right of a modern house to a hedge gap onto the B4031 in the far corner of the field.

Turn right onto this road and after nearly 300 yards turn left onto bridleway DD21, the macadam drive to Tomwell Farm, with views of Deddington to your left and across the next valley towards Duns Tew ahead. About 150 yards beyond the first hedge to your right, look out for a rail stile in the left-hand hedge. Here leave the drive and bear half right onto path DD9 aiming left of Over Worton Church in trees on the other side of the valley to a hedge gap about 100 yards left of the field corner. Now bear half right across the next field heading for Over Worton Church to pass through a hedge gap, then bear half left across the third field to a stile and footbridge in the bottom hedge between clumps of tree. Bear half left across the fourth field to cross a footbridge and stile in a hedge gap, then bear half right across the fifth to a hedge gap some way left of an oak tree then keep straight on to a stile onto a road just right of a gap in the trees ahead.

Turn left onto this road crossing Ilbury Bridge then at a road junction turn right onto the road to Nether Worton. At a left-hand bend where the road was formerly gated, go through the old gateway then turn left through a gate onto path WR6. Now turn right and follow the back of the roadside hedge to cross some rails under an oak tree then bear half left across a field towards a cottage on a hillside ahead to reach the back hedge of the field where you turn right and follow the hedge to a white gate in the field corner. Go through this then bear half right across a field to cross a wooden fence left of a clump of trees and a white gate to enter the left-hand of two fields ahead. Now bear half left across this field to a white gate left of a double-pole pylon in the far corner. Here turn left onto one of the few remaining gated roads in Oxfordshire passing through a gate then bear half right again onto path WR6 leaving the road and heading for the left-hand end of a copse with a view of Worton House to your left. When Over Worton Church comes into view ahead, go straight towards it crossing a wooden fence and reaching a gate into the churchyard.

If wishing to visit the church, rebuilt in Victorian times but retaining a thirteenth-century chancel arch and some mediaeval glass, go through the gate. Otherwise turn sharp right onto path WR1 following a left-hand fence downhill with a fine view across the valley ahead. Where a hedge begins, bear slightly right diverging from it to reach a hunting gate in the bottom hedge. Go through this and bear half left across a field corner to cross a culvert and stile, then continue across the next field to a stile 100 yards right of its far corner. Here go straight across the next field heading for a clump of tall trees left of Manor Farm to cross a stile and join a road. Turn left onto this road and follow it through Nether Worton passing its tiny church which was largely rebuilt in 1630 but incorporates a thirteenth-century doorway.

At a T-junction, where the seventeenth-century Nether Worton House can be seen to your left, turn right onto the Barford and Bloxham road. Follow this for some 300 yards to a sharp left-hand bend then leave the road crossing the entrance to a concrete road and going through a white gate onto path WR9. Now bear slightly left over the top of a rise, aiming for the gap between Steepness Hill and

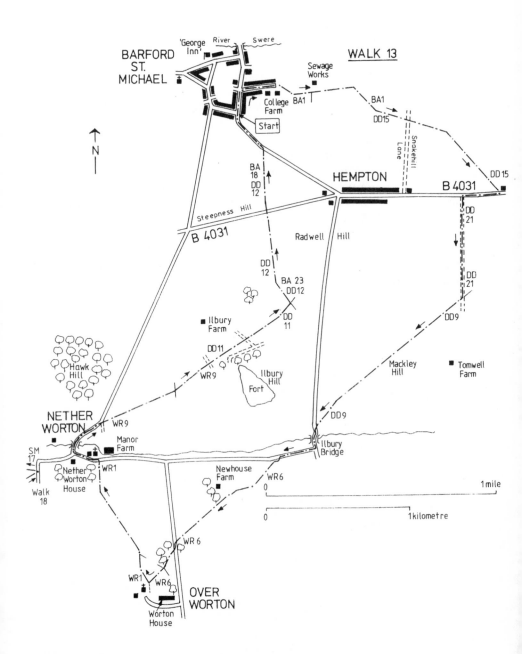

WALK 13

'George Inn'   River   Swere

BARFORD
ST.
MICHAEL

Sewage
Works

BA1   BA1

College   DD15
Farm

Start

N

BA
18
DD
12

HEMPTON   B 4031

DD 15

Steepness Hill   DD
21

B 4031   Radwell   Hill

DD
21

DD
12   DD
9

BA 23
DD12

DD
11   Ilbury
Farm

DD11   Mackley
Hill   Tomwell
Farm

WR9   Ilbury
Hill
Fort

Hawk
Hill

NETHER
WORTON   DD9

WR 9   Ilbury
Bridge

Manor
Farm

SM
17   Newhouse
Farm   WR6

Nether   0   1mile
Worton   WR1
House

Walk
18   0   1kilometre

WR 6

WR1   WR6

OVER
WORTON

Worton
House

79

Ilbury Hill ahead when these come into view, to reach a stile in a hedge ahead. Here go straight on to reach the end of a hedge, then bear slightly left, aiming for the gap between the hills again, to cross a gated farm bridge. Now take path DD11 straight on with Ilbury Hill with its Iron Age hill fort to your right, crossing a track and stile and gradually diverging from the right-hand hedge, crossing another track and heading for a gate just left of a clump of trees ahead. DO NOT go through the gate but cross a stile to the right of it, then bear half left heading towards a building in a hollow ahead. After about 150 yards in the middle of the field turn left onto path DD12 (later BA23) to a hedge gap in its top left-hand corner, then follow the left-hand hedge uphill. Where the hedge turns left, take path DD12 straight on across the field to a gateway onto the B4031 at the top of Steepness Hill. Bear slightly left across this road to go through a hedge gap virtually opposite then take path DD12 (later BA18) following a right-hand hedge downhill through three fields to reach a road into Barford St. Michael. Turn left onto this and follow it to your starting point.

WALK 14 : CROPREDY

Length of Walk:	(A) 8.5 miles / 13.6 Km
	(B) 7.1 miles / 11.4 Km
Starting Point:	'Brasenose Arms', Cropredy.
Grid Ref:	SP468465
Maps:	OS Landranger Sheet 151
	OS Pathfinder Sheet 1022 (SP44/54)

How to get there / Parking: Cropredy, 4 miles north of Banbury, may be reached from the town or M40 Jct.11 by taking the A361 towards Daventry for 2–3 miles then turning left onto a road signposted to Williamscot, Cropredy and Great Bourton and following it for 1.2 miles to Cropredy. At a triangular green fork right, joining the Mollington and Claydon road by the 'Brasenose Arms'. Take the next turning right at another small green and find a suitable place to park.

Notes: Some parts of the walk may become flooded after heavy rain.

Cropredy on the banks of the Oxford Canal and River Cherwell in the northern most tip of Oxfordshire is best known for the Battle of Cropredy Bridge which took place just east of the village in June 1644 when Charles I took the strategically important bridge over the Cherwell from the Parliamentarian general, Sir William Waller. Relics of this battle can be found in the fourteenth-century parish church as can a mediaeval brass lectern in the shape of an eagle which was hidden in the river during the Civil War. Locally pronounced 'Crupdy', the village with its attractive ironstone and brick thatched cottages became prosperous following the arrival of the Oxford Canal in the 1770s and in more recent times was home to the late Labour cabinet minister and diarist, Richard Crossman.

Both walks take you from Cropredy across the canal and river before climbing gently to Wardington and the lofty ridge above it on the Northamptonshire boundary. Walk B then drops directly into Upper Wardington, while Walk A continues along the ridge to take full advantage of its views, before both descend gently to the Northamptonshire village of Chacombe, site of a mediaeval priory.

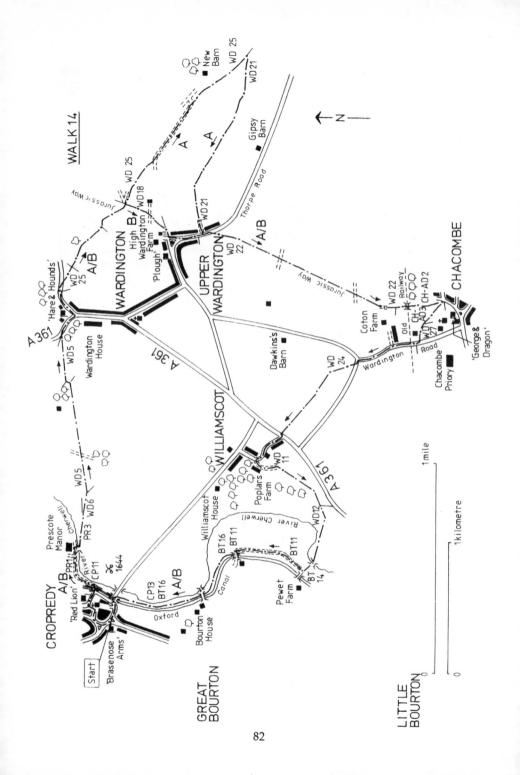

WALK 14

82

The return route takes you by way of the pretty hamlet of Williamscot before descending Williamscot Hill with fine views across the Cherwell valley and following the canal towpath back to Cropredy.

Both walks start from the 'Brasenose Arms', Cropredy and take Station Road towards Mollington and Claydon. By a small green turn right then turn right again into Church Lane. At its far end go through gates into the churchyard then turn left along a concrete path by a stone wall to gates into Red Lion Street. Turn right here passing the church and the 'Red Lion'. At a road junction take the Prescote road (path CP11) straight on over a canal bridge then bearing left and joining the banks of the Cherwell. Having crossed a bridge, the road (now path PR1) continues towards Prescote Manor. Where the road forks, take a concrete road straight on through gates. After about 90 yards turn right onto path PR3 crossing a bridge over the Cherwell then turning left through a kissing-gate. Follow the Cherwell straight on then, where it bears left, keep straight on across the corner of a field to cross a stile and bridge. Now take path WD6 aiming for the middle of a plantation at the far end of the field. Halfway across the field, level with a hedge junction to your right, bear half left onto path WD5 to cross a footbridge under a crabtree. Now bear half right across a corner of the next field to a gate by a lightning-damaged ash tree. Here keep straight on across two more fields to reach the right-hand end of a plantation on a hillside ahead with views opening out behind you towards Cropredy and Great Bourton. Now follow the outside edge of the plantation straight on to a gate then bear slightly right across the next field aiming for the left-hand end of a copse ahead with views of Wardington to your right and towards Claydon and Chipping Warden to your left to reach a red gate onto the A361.

Turn right and follow this road carefully into Wardington. Before reaching a blind bend and junction by the 'Hare and Hounds', cross the road, then at this junction turn left onto the Edgcote road and follow it out of the village rounding a right-hand bend. Where the road starts to bend to the left, turn right through an iron gate onto path WD25 then immediately left through a second gate. Now bear half right across a field to a tall oak at the top of the rise. By the oak tree turn right and follow a left-hand fence, later a hedge uphill along the Northamptonshire boundary through four fields to the top of the hill with wide views behind particularly in the second and third fields.

In the fourth field at the top of the hill by a gate and stile in the left-hand hedge where there are wide views to your right over Wardington with its thirteenth-century church towards Middleton Cheney, Banbury and beyond, **Walk B** turns right onto path WD18 (part of the Jurassic Way), descending to the left-hand of two gates then bearing slightly right across the next field towards a yellow-painted gable end at Upper Wardington to reach a stile. Now follow an enclosed path straight on, joining a drive and following it to a road. Turn left onto this joining Thorpe Road and taking it straight on to rejoin **Walk A**. Now omit the next paragraph.

Walk A continues along path WD25 following the left-hand hedge and county boundary for nearly a further mile with wide views to your right towards Middleton Cheney, Banbury and beyond, passing through a gate and two further fields. At the far end of the second field turn sharp right onto path WD21 crossing the field diagonally to join the bottom hedge left of an oak tree then bearing right and following the hedge to a corner of the field. Here go through a hedge gap crossing a ditch and a rail stile then follow the left-hand hedge for about 100 yards. Where the hedge begins to bear left, leave it and follow a line of trees straight on to cross a rail stile at the corner of a fence left of a gate. Now follow a right-hand hedge straight on through two fields to cross a rail stile at the far end of the second field. Here bear half left and follow a right-hand hedge to a gate into a short green lane leading to Thorpe Road at Upper Wardington, onto which you turn left rejoining **Walk B**.

Opposite the third pair of council houses to your left **Walks A and B** turn right through a kissing-gate by a gate onto path WD22 (part of the Jurassic Way) and bear half left across a field to a pair of gates left of the far corner. Go through these and follow a right-hand hedge straight on with views towards Middleton Cheney ahead. At the far end of the field cross a stile and go straight on across a field to cross a track and further stile then continue, with Chacombe coming into view in the valley ahead and views across Banbury further to your right, to two stiles left of a gate. Cross these and follow a right-hand hedge straight on to cross a stile by a gate and a track at the far end of the field. Here continue across a field with pronounced ridges and furrows indicating mediaeval cultivation to a gate and stile left of the field corner. Now follow a left-hand fence straight on past an old orchard to a further gate and stile, then follow a right-hand fence straight on to a rail stile leading to a bridge under the former Banbury–Woodford Halse railway opened in 1900 and closed in 1966. Pass under this bridge then cross a track and take the fenced path to a footbridge and stile at the Northamptonshire boundary. Here take path CH–AD2 straight on over a further footbridge then uphill to gates onto a road opposite the right-hand end of a thatched cottage at Chacombe.

Chacombe, sometimes spelt Chalcombe, was the site of an Augustinian priory founded by Hugh Chacombe in the twelfth century. The fourteenth-century church with its Norman font to your right, some earthworks and part of the house known as Chacombe Priory, which was restored after a fire in 1600, are all that now remains of what must have been a major religious establishment.

If wishing to seek refreshment or explore the village, go through these gates. Otherwise turn sharp right onto path CH–AD3 passing right of some of the priory earthworks and the church and continuing to a footbridge in the bottom corner of the field. Here go straight on to cross some rails and a further footbridge at the county boundary. Now take path WD27 bearing slightly left across a field passing left of a cottage garden to reach a stile in the far corner of the field leading to Wardington Road. Turn right onto this road and follow it passing between former railway embankments then climbing for a quarter mile and ignoring an unsignposted side-turning to your right, to reach a road junction. Here fork left onto the Williamscot and Banbury road then after about 25 yards turn right through a former gateway onto path WD24 bearing half left across a field to cross a footbridge at the corner of a hedge. Now follow a left-hand hedge straight on through two fields to reach the A361.

Cross this and take a side road straight on into Williamscot. At a sharp right-hand bend by the entrance to Poplars Farm, turn left through a gate onto path WD11 passing through three further gates into a field with pronounced ridges and furrows. Now take a grassy track beside a left-hand fence straight on to a corner of the field with views towards Banbury ahead and across the Cherwell valley towards the Bourtons to your right. Here bear right and follow a left-hand hedge downhill to a gate into another field with ridges and furrows. Bear slightly right across this field joining bridleway WD12 and reaching a gate in the bottom hedge. Now bear slightly right across the next field, with views of Williamscot House to your right in places, to cross a bridge over the River Cherwell by a willow tree. Williamscot House, built by Walter Calcott in 1568, boasts having played host to Charles I on the night after his victory at Cropredy Bridge.

Now take bridleway BT14 bearing slightly right across a field towards a brick bridge over the Oxford Canal. Do NOT cross this bridge but turn right onto bridleway BT11 following a raised causeway beside the canal-side hedge to your left through three fields to another bridge. Do NOT cross this either but go through a gate, then turn left over a stile and descend a slope onto the canal towpath (BT16). Turn right onto this passing under the bridge and following the towpath for two-thirds of a mile, going under another bridge, passing Bourton House, a brick manor house to your left and (now as path CP13) approaching a third bridge. Here fork right off the towpath to a small gate onto a road on the edge of Cropredy then turn left onto it crossing a bridge and continuing straight on to reach the 'Brasenose Arms'.

WALK 15: WROXTON

Length of Walk:	8.5 miles / 13.7 Km
Starting Point:	Wroxton village pond.
Grid Ref:	SP414418
Maps:	OS Landranger Sheet 151
	OS Pathfinder Sheets 1021 (SP24/34),
	1022 (SP44/54), 1044 (SP23/33)
	& 1045 (SP43/53)

How to get there / parking: Wroxton, 2.5 miles west of Banbury, may be reached from the town by taking the A422 westwards. On entering the village, at a sharp right-hand bend near the 'Wroxton House Hotel', take a side road straight on towards the church bearing right and passing the 'North Arms' to park either by the entrance to Wroxton College or on the wide section of the village street near the pond.

Wroxton, with its picturesque thatched ironstone cottages around a small green and pond, must be one of the prettiest villages in Oxfordshire. In 1666 much of the village was destroyed in a major fire but its fourteenth-century church and Wroxton Abbey survived. The church contains monuments to Sir William Pope and his wife, various members of the North family and Thomas Coutts, founder of the well-known Coutts Bank. Wroxton Abbey (now Wroxton College) was acquired by Sir Thomas Pope, founder of Trinity College, Oxford, during the Reformation. His descendant, Sir William Pope built the present house on the site of this former Augustinian priory in 1618. In 1744 its park was landscaped by Sanderson Miller for Lord North who represented Banbury in Parliament from 1754 to 1790 and from 1770 to 1782 was Prime Minister. It was, indeed, during his term that Britain lost her American colonies and this was seen as largely his responsibility, so it is perhaps somewhat ironic that his country seat should now belong to an American university!

The walk, which is one of great interest and variety, not only leads you through Wroxton Park, but also traverses Broughton Park with good views of its mediaeval castle. It then proceeds westwards

WALK 15

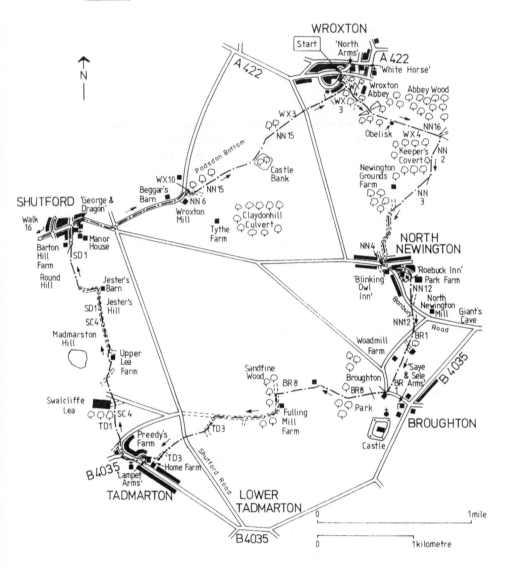

WROXTON

Start   'North Arms'

A 422   A 422   'White Horse'

Wroxton Abbey   Abbey Wood

WX 3   WX 3

N

WX 3   NN 15   Obelisk   WX 4   NN 16

Podsdon Bottom   Castle Bank   Keeper's Covert   NN 2

WX 10   NN 15   Newington Grounds Farm   NN 3

Beggar's Barn   NN 6

Wroxton Mill   Claydonhill Culvert

SHUTFORD   'George & Dragon'   Tythe Farm   NN 4   NORTH NEWINGTON

Walk 16   Manor House   'Roebuck Inn'   Park Farm

Barton Hill Farm   SD 1   'Blinking Owl Inn'   NN 12   North Newington Mill   Giant's Cave

Round Hill   Jester's Barn   NN 12   BR 1

SD 1   Jester's Hill   Woadmill Farm   Banbury Road

SC 4

Madmarston Hill   Upper Lea Farm   Sandfine Wood   BR 8   Broughton   Saye & Sele BR Arms   B 4035

Swalcliffe Lea   SC 4   Fulling Mill Farm   BR 8   Park   BROUGHTON

TD 1   Preedy's Farm   TD 3   Castle

Lampet Arms'   TD 3   Home Farm   Shutford Road

B 4035   LOWER TADMARTON

TADMARTON

B 4035

0   1mile

0   1kilometre

into the remote hills around Tadmarton and Shutford with fine views in places and passes close to Iron Age earthworks on Madmarston Hill and at Castle Bank before returning to Wroxton.

Starting by Wroxton's beautiful village pond, cross Main Street and take Dark Lane right of the entrance to Wroxton College. At a right-hand bend turn left onto fenced path WX4 left of a gravel drive. Follow it, ignoring a private crossing path, to a kissing-gate into a parkland field where there is a folly in the form of a castellated tower ahead. Here bear left and follow a worn path past the ironstone Jacobean Abbey, gradually diverging from the left-hand fence to reach a gate and kissing-gate. Now bear half left passing left of a clump of trees and bushes concealing a pond and descending to a gate left of a lake. Take a fenced path straight on between lakes to a stile then bear slightly left uphill passing left of a copse and heading just left of an obelisk to cross a rail stile where there is a fine view behind you of the Abbey and its garden. Now bear slightly right passing just left of the obelisk then, with a view towards the edge of Banbury on the skyline ahead, continue downhill (later on path NN16) to reach the bottom corner of the field.

Here ignore a bridge ahead and turn right onto path NN2 entering the next field. Bear half right across it to the middle of a wood called Keeper's Covert then turn left and follow its outside edge to a corner. Keep straight on to a large sycamore tree then bear half right onto path NN3 crossing the field diagonally to an oak tree by the corner of a hedge. Now go straight on to the far corner of the field by another wood. Here join a farm track, soon bearing left and following the track over the hill into North Newington.

At the edge of the village the track bears right joining path NN4 then bears left to reach the village street. Turn left onto this, immediately forking right to pass right of the village green and in front of the 'Blinking Owl Inn', then fork left into Park Lane. Where the road wiggles to the right and narrows, turn right onto path NN12 between a fence and a stone shed and follow it to a stile into a field where there is a fine stone dovecote at Park Farm to your left. Bear slightly left across the parkland field passing right of a chestnut tree to reach a gap in a stone wall where the farm drive joins Banbury Road. Cross this road bearing half left over a stile and along a grass cropbreak to a gateway and a stile onto another road where

Broughton comes into view ahead. Turn right onto this road, then immediately left over a stile onto path BR1 bearing half right across a field towards the spire of Broughton Church to reach a stile in the far corner of the field. Cross this, the sewage works drive and a footbridge opposite then bear slightly left, still heading towards Broughton Church, to reach a gate onto a road opposite a lodge of Broughton Castle.

Broughton Castle and the nearby church were both built by Thomas de Broughton in about 1300 and his well-preserved tomb together with several monuments to the Fiennes family are amongst the most interesting features of the church. The moated castle was later sold to William of Wykeham whose descendants through marriage, the Fiennes family, now the Lords Saye & Sele, still live there today. In the sixteenth century the castle was extended and converted into an Elizabethan manor house, but it retains many features of the original building including its chapel and fifteenth-century gatehouse. Broughton Castle played a major role in the Civil War as William Fiennes, the first Lord Saye & Sele, was one of the leaders of the Parliamentary side. Meetings attended by John Pym, John Hampden, Sir Henry Vane and the Earl of Essex were held in its secret room; it was once besieged by Royalist forces and William Fiennes raised his own regiment known as Lord Saye's Bluecoats who fought at Edgehill. Fiennes, who opposed the execution of Charles I, however, proved his nickname of 'Old Subtlety' to be justified by ingratiating himself with Charles II to the extent that Charles made him Lord Privy Seal prior to his death in 1662.

Bear right across the road and a stone stile onto path BR8 entering Broughton Park. Now go straight ahead across the park passing right of the first pair of trees and two of a group of three small trees with protective fencing, with fine views to your left of the church and moated castle, making sure you do not cross a shallow sunken way which should stay some yards to your left. On eventually reaching the near right-hand corner of a copse, keep straight on through a hunting-gate and across a field to cross a stile by a gate just left of a Dutch Barn. Now bear half right and follow a right-hand hedge, later a fence, through two fields to a gate onto a rough road.

Turn left onto this road and follow it downhill past Fulling Mill Farm then over a stream and on to a gate into a field. Here take a grassy track gradually bearing right and joining the right-hand edge of a beech copse. Now go through a gate and follow the track straight on uphill through two more fields with wide views to your right. Near the far end of the second field, turn left onto path TD3, a grassy track following a right-hand hedge with wide views to your left. Where the track bears left, leave it and bear right through a hedge gap and across a field with views towards Tadmarton ahead, to reach a small hedge gap onto Shutford Road some 50 yards right of an ash tree. Bear half left through a gate virtually opposite and go straight on across a field heading right of some barns at Tadmarton to enter a slightly sunken track at a gap in the next hedge. Follow it downhill to cross a bridge over a stream then bear right across a field aiming for the gable end of a cottage right of a row of thatched cottages. Cross a rail stile by the cottage then turn left then right onto a macadam lane which you follow, soon bearing left to reach the B4035 by the 'Lampet Arms' in Tadmarton.

Cross this road and turn right onto its pavement passing the Norman church with its tall tower completed in the fifteenth century, then continuing behind a roadside hedge. On reaching a large chestnut tree, turn right down some stone steps, cross the B4035 and take the Swalcliffe Lea road. Having rounded a right-hand bend, turn left over a stile onto path TD1 crossing some rails in the right-hand hedge and bearing slightly left across a field towards the right-hand end of a greenhouse on a hillside ahead to reach a footbridge and stile. Cross these and take path SC4 following a left-hand tree-belt, then a hedge uphill between two ponds, past an orchard and through a field to a hedge gap onto the drive to Swalcliffe Lea.

Cross this and go through a small gate opposite, then go straight on to a narrow road by a disused stile. Here bear slightly left across the next field to the far corner with views of Swalcliffe Church, parts of which date from Saxon times, to your left. Now turn right onto a grassy track passing through a gate then fork immediately left through a hedge gap and follow a left-hand hedge through the old orchard of Upper Lea Farm. By a concrete stable turn left through a gate then turn right skirting the farm buildings, but passing right of a new barn, with views of Madmarston Hill capped by its Iron Age hill fort to your left, and joining a stony track. Follow this beside a right-hand hedge up the side of Jester's Hill. At the far end of the field go through the right-hand of two gates onto path SD1, still following the stony track to a gate near Jester's Barn then turning left to reach a hedge gap by an oak tree. Go through this then bear half right across a field to cross a footbridge and stile right of an oak tree. Now go straight on with fine views of Shutford Manor House to your right to reach gates onto a village street at Shutford, until 1948 location of a factory supplying plush to various royal houses including for the coronation of Nicholas II, the last Russian czar, in 1894.

Take this road straight on past the Norman Church with its fifteenth-century pinnacled tower on the top of a steep bank. At a crossroads by the 'George and Dragon' turn right onto the Banbury road leaving the village. At a five-way junction bear half left onto the Wroxton and Hanwell road and follow it for half a mile dropping into a valley. Having passed the thatched Wroxton Mill, turn right between white gateposts onto fenced bridleway WX10 and follow it through a gate into a green lane (bridleway NN6) which gradually bears left and soon emerges into a field. Here take path NN15 straight on through a gate bearing slightly right uphill to join the top hedge. Follow this above Padsdon Bottom to the far end of the field, then cross some rails and go straight on to join the edge of a tree belt concealing Iron Age earthworks known as Castle Bank. Now bear slightly left and follow the tree belt later a hedge passing two gates to reach a stile. Having crossed this stile, bear half left across a field to a hedge gap right of a sycamore tree, then take path WX3 straight on across the next field to a hedge gap in the far corner. Here cross a road and a stile opposite where Wroxton comes into view ahead, then follow a right-hand fence straight on. At the far end of the field turn right through gates, then left over a stile and follow the right-hand fence to another stile. Now continue beside a line of trees to a small gate onto fenced path WX4. Follow this to a village street then turn right for your starting point.

WALK 16 :   SHENINGTON

Length of Walk: 6.4 miles / 10.4 Km
Starting Point: 'Bell Inn', Shenington.
Grid Ref: SP372428
Maps: OS Landranger Sheet 151
           OS Pathfinder Sheets 1021 (SP24/34)
           & 1044 (SP23/33)
How to get there / Parking: Shenington, some 5 miles northwest
    of Banbury, may be reached from the town by taking the
    A422 for 4.6 miles through Wroxton towards Stratford-upon-
    Avon, then forking left onto a road signposted to Alkerton
    and Shenington and following it for 1.2 miles to Shenington
    village green where you find a suitable place to park.

Shenington and its twin village of Alkerton in the remote
north-west corner of Oxfordshire with their stone cottages and
pretty gardens often on sloping ground, but for the use of the local
ironstone of the North Oxfordshire Redlands, are fine examples of
what one expects of a Cotswold village. Shenington, most of which
is on a hilltop, is the larger village with its inn, cottages and
twelfth-century church with a fifteenth-century embattled tower
ranged around a lush, well-kept village green, while tiny Alkerton,
spread along a steep hillside, can boast another Norman church and
a Jacobean rectory. Both villages are located on the D'Arcy Dalton
Way, a long-distance path opened by the Society in 1987 to
commemorate our founder member and late President, Colonel
W. P. D'Arcy Dalton. This route links the county's four main
long-distance paths – the Ridgeway Path, Thames Path, Oxfordshire
Way and Oxford Canal Towpath and so enables them to be
combined in long-distance circuits. In so doing the D'Arcy Dalton
Way connects some of the most remote and beautiful tracts of
countryside on the western edge of the county and so provides a
superb five-day walk in its own right.

    The walk described here explores the quiet countryside to the
south of Shenington and Alkerton, first following the valley which
separates them southwards to Shutford then heading west for the

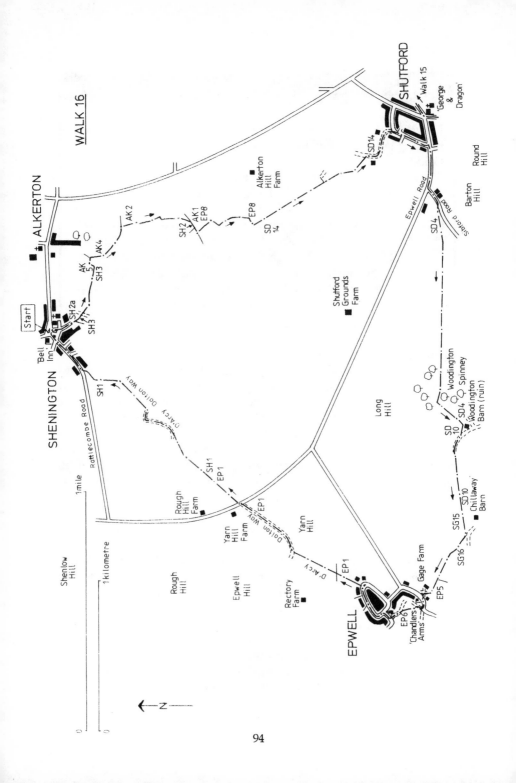

WALK 16

94

upland plateau around Epwell which is punctuated by strange-looking single largely treeless hills, some of which are over 700 feet high, before taking the D'Arcy Dalton Way back to Shenington.

Starting from the 'Bell Inn' at Shenington, cross the major road and take a small road straight on across the village green to enter a lane at the back right-hand corner of the green. Where the road ends, take path SH2a straight on through a gate into a green lane. On reaching a large lawn, go straight on over a stone stile and a rail stile into a field and bear half left onto path SH3 with a fine view of Alkerton ahead, descending steeply and crossing a concrete road to reach a gate in the bottom corner of the field. Go through this, then turn left through a hedge gap and bear slightly right across the next field to a rail stile in the bottom hedge leading to a footbridge. Cross this and take path AK5 through a gate into an immaculately maintained garden, bearing half left to pass left of a chestnut tree and through a shrubbery then up a bank to a stile. Here turn right onto enclosed path AK4 passing through a gate then going straight on across a lawn to a gate into a field.

Now keep straight on, joining a left-hand hedge and following it to a field corner. Here ignore a hedge gap ahead and turn right onto path AK2 following a left-hand hedge downhill to a stile. Cross this, a concealed sleeper footbridge and a second stile then follow a right-hand fence through three fields, soon joining a hedge and a stream. (If obstructed at the end of the third field, use a stile some 40 yards to your left.) On entering the fourth field, continue for about 70 yards then just past a stunted hawthorn tree turn right onto bridleway AK1 crossing a culvert.

Now go through a bridlegate and bear half left onto bridleway SH2 across a field to a bridlebridge and gate. Cross the bridge then turn left onto path EP8 following a left-hand hedge. After about 30 yards go straight on across the corner of the field to rejoin and follow the left-hand hedge to the far end of the field. Here turn right, then after some 70 yards turn left over a stile and footbridge onto path SD14 and go straight across a field to double gates in the top hedge. Go through these and follow a left-hand hedge straight on. Where it turns left, bear slightly right across the field to go through double gates in the far hedge. In the next field bear slightly right heading about 50 yards right of a tall ash tree in the far hedge to pass through a hedge gap, then keep straight on down a marshy field to a rail-stile and footbridge at the bottom. Cross these and bear slightly right climbing to cross a rail stile in the top hedge. Now bear half left to cross a stile in the left-hand hedge by a small ash tree. Turn right here into a green lane. Just past a barn at a junction of tracks turn left into another green lane, soon turning right to reach a village street in Shutford, once centre of the plush-making industry supplying royal houses across Europe.

Turn right onto this road and follow it straight on past a small village green to a T-junction. Here turn right into Epwell Road leaving Shutford. After about 350 yards at a road junction turn left onto the Sibfords and Hook Norton road. Just past a small cemetery turn right over a stile by a gate onto path SD4 bearing left and joining a right-hand hedge, then follow this hedge straight on through three fields. At the far end of the third field go through a hedge gap and straight on across the next field with a view to your left towards Swalcliffe, passing the bottom end of a hillside copse and the right-hand end of a second copse called Woodington Spinney then continuing to a gap in the left-hand hedge. Go through this then bear slightly left across another field to cross a ditch and fence at the left-hand end of a hedge right of the ruins of Woodington Barn. (If the path is still obstructed here, turn left past the ruins, then right onto a grassy track and right again through gates to rejoin the official route of the walk).

Now take bridleway SD10 bearing half right across a rough field to a bridlegate by an electricity pole. Here go straight on over a footbridge by a ford and across a field to the corner of a hedge then follow this left-hand hedge to a gate at the far end of the field. Take bridleway SG15 straight on through this and follow a right-hand hedge past a farm known as Chillaway Barn to reach a gate near a farm road. Go through this and bear slightly right onto bridleway SG16 following a right-hand hedge for a quarter mile to pass through a bridlegate. Joining the D'Arcy Dalton Way, take bridleway EP5 still following the right-hand hedge. Disregard a gate in the hedge and follow a right-hand fence straight on past Gage Farm to a gate leading onto its drive. Go through the gate and join the drive then turn left onto a crossing drive to reach a village street in Epwell.

Turn left onto this road passing the 'Chandlers Arms' then fork right onto a drive and turn right again onto path EP6 through the pub car park onto a grassy track. On entering a field, bear half left across it to the end of a hedge where you rejoin the grassy track entering a green lane and continuing past the tiny thirteenth-century church, once a chapel-of-ease of Swalcliffe, to reach another road. Turn right onto this then at a T-junction turn left onto a village street which gradually bears right. On reaching a sharp right-hand bend, go straight on past Horseshoe Cottage then bear half left onto path EP1 taking a drive through a gate then keeping straight on through a garden to reach a stone footbridge. Cross this and bear slightly left to join a left-hand hedge at a rail stile, then follow it straight on through four fields passing between Epwell Hill and Yarn Hill to reach a road near Yarn Hill Farm.

Turn left onto this road then after about 30 yards turn right over a stile (still on path EP1) and cross a field diagonally to an electricity pole then keep straight on to cross a stile and footbridge left of the far corner of the field. Now take path SH1 bearing half right across a field, climbing steeply at first then crossing a ridge to reach a gate left of the far corner of the field. Go through this then turn right and follow a right-hand hedge to a footbridge, then gradually diverge from the hedge to cross a stile right of an iron gate. Now take a grassy track round the foot of a hill to a gate in the far corner of the field, then bear half right across the next field climbing steeply to a bridlegate. Go through this and follow a right-hand hedge straight on to cross some rails by a gate. Here bear half left downhill to cross a footbridge at the left-hand end of a line of willows, then follow a right-hand fence uphill to a rail stile onto Rattlecombe Road on the edge of Shenington. Turn right onto this road and follow it to your starting point.

WALK 17 :   HOOK NORTON

Length of Walk: 8.3 miles / 13.3 Km
Starting Point: 'Bell Inn', Hook Norton.
Grid Ref: SP356331
Maps: OS Landranger Sheet 151
OS Pathfinder Sheet 1044 (SP23/33)
How to get there / Parking: Hook Norton, 7.5 miles southwest
of Banbury, may be reached from the town by taking the
A361 towards Chipping Norton for 4 miles. Having passed
through Bloxham, turn right onto a road signposted to
Milcombe, Wigginton and Hook Norton and follow it for
4 miles to Hook Norton. In the village take the winding
priority road until you reach the 'Bell Inn' on your right,
just past which there is a parking area on your left.
Notes: In 1992 this walk had several serious obstructions but
it is hoped that these will now have been resolved.

Hook Norton, locally called 'Hookey', is probably best known today
for its brewery, one of the smallest in the country. Indeed some
50 years ago it was a hive of industry with, in addition to the
brewery, an ironworks, active ironstone quarries and the
Banbury–Cheltenham railway crossing the valley on an 80-feet-high
viaduct. However today the ironworks and railway have closed and
the pillars of the viaduct and quarry faces are rapidly disappearing
beneath rampant tree cover, so that this large Redland village in its
quiet valley with a wealth of fine stone cottages dominated by an
impressive Perpendicular church tower, when seen from the
surrounding hills, appears to have descended into an enchanted
slumber.

The walk explores the remote hills to the east of the village where
fine views abound, taking you first over a ridge to the picturesque
village of Swerford before following the slopes of the Swere valley
to the ancient hillside village of Wigginton. Having crossed another
ridge, you climb to the heights of Wigginton Heath before
descending with fine views back into Hook Norton.

Starting from the 'Bell Inn' in Hook Norton, go down Bell Hill to a small green then turn left into Park Road. At another road junction go straight on, then at a sharp left-hand bend bear half right onto macadamed bridleway HN23. Take it up hill out of the village, levelling out and passing between pillars of the old railway viaduct, built in 1887 and demolished some years after its closure in 1951. Just past a right-hand bungalow called 'Little Orchis' turn right through a gate onto path HN25 bearing half left across a paddock to cross a stile. Here bear half right passing right of an oak tree and descending a steep bank to cross a bridge over a stream. Now ignore a stile in a fence ahead and turn right following a left-hand fence through the scrub. On emerging into a field, bear slightly right diverging from the left-hand hedge and passing through a gap in scrubland covering old quarry workings. Now keep straight on to a corner of a hedge then follow this left-hand hedge uphill with a fine view of Hook Norton and the old railway viaduct behind, to cross a stile in the top corner of the field. Here continue beside a left-hand hedge with further fine views behind. At the far end of the field go through a hedge gap and keep straight on with wide views of the Swere valley and Swerford opening out ahead passing right of a concrete water installation to reach a farm road by a tall sycamore. Turn left onto this passing between gateposts then turn right descending across a field to pass through a gap at a corner of a hedge. Now follow the right-hand hedge to a concealed gap in it with redundant stile steps leading to a road.

Turn left onto this road. After 25 yards turn right over a stile (currently overgrown) and take path HN25 bearing slightly left towards Swerford Church to cross a wooden fence at the bottom left-hand corner of the field. Here continue towards the church crossing stiles in two further fences and descending steps to cross a footbridge over the Swere and a stile. Now take path SW13 bearing slightly right across a field to a culvert then bear half left to a gate and stile in the top left-hand corner of the field into a green lane straight on uphill to the village street in Swerford Church End.

Turn left onto this road, bearing slightly left, crossing a small village green and passing the thirteenth-century church with its stone steeple and some fourteenth-century glass, behind which are earthworks marking the site of a Norman castle. Just past a stone bungalow to your right fork right through a gate onto path SW10 bearing slightly right across a parkland field to a gate in a dip then keep straight on with views of a fine stone farmhouse to your left to reach the far right-hand corner of the field where there is a wide view down the Swere valley towards Wigginton and Milcombe. Here cross a stile then turn left over a second stile onto path SW6 following a left-hand hedge to a stile in it. Cross this then ignore a branching path to your left and take a fenced path straight on. Having passed a cottage, turn left onto a gravel track (byway SW19) and follow it downhill through two gates passing a cottage to reach the village street in Swerford East End.

Take this road downhill across a green, then at a sharp left-hand bend by a telephone box take a rough macadam road straight on towards some cottages. Where the road turns right towards a farmyard, leave it and take path SW2 straight on along an alleyway between the cottages to a stile into a field. Here turn right onto path SW3 passing a barn to your right, going through two gates and continuing along a fenced grassy track with fine views of the Swere valley. At the far end of the field go through the right-hand of two hedge gaps and follow a left-hand hedge to a gate under an oak tree. Here continue across the next field, heading for Hailcombe Barn on Bury's Hill ahead, to reach a gate and culvert in the next hedge. Now go straight on across two further fields with views of Wigginton Church ahead, crossing a footbridge and reaching a hedge gap at the left-hand end of a row of trees on the Wigginton road.

Cross this road and two stiles opposite then take path SW4 bearing half left across a field, crossing two wooden fences and continuing to a gate near the far hedge. Go through this and take path SN12 straight on through a hedge gap then between a fence and a left-hand hedge to a stile into a spinney. Keep straight on through the spinney to reach a farm road then turn left crossing the farm road and a stile and taking a permissive path through a plantation to another stile. Now follow a right-hand fence to a corner of the field then turn left onto path SN13 following a right-hand hedge over a hill. In a field corner go straight on over a stile and a set of rails then turn right and follow a right-hand hedge with fine views of Wigginton to your left. Where the hedge bears right, leave it and keep straight on to cross a footbridge over a grassy stream at the far end of the field. Now bear half right to a second footbridge onto a road on the edge of Wigginton.

The attractive ironstone village of Wigginton is a settlement of ancient origin as the site of a substantial Roman villa was discovered near the church in 1824 and the village's name is of Anglo-Saxon origin. The thirteenth-century church with its fifteenth-century tower containing some Roman bricks, which had to be substantially restored in 1870 when it is said to have been dangerous, is also believed to be on the site of an earlier building.

Turn left onto this road and follow it over the River Swere bridge, past The Old Watermill then uphill into the village. Now disregard a turning to your left and go straight on past the church then bear left, ignoring a turning to the right, to reach a T-junction in the centre of the village. Here turn right soon reaching another T-junction near the 'White Swan'. Turn right again onto the Hook Norton and Tadmarton road and follow it for nearly half a mile over a hill with fine views to left and right in places. On reaching a crossroads, turn left onto the Hook Norton road. After a third of a mile at a left-hand bend, turn right through a gate onto path WG8 following a green lane over the old railway line into a field. Now take a grassy track straight on to a hedge gap. Bear slightly left across the next field to a gateway in its top hedge just left of Withycoombe Farm then keep straight on across the corner of the next field towards a bungalow at the farm to reach a gate by an electricity pole. Go through this gate and turn right through a second gate into the bungalow garden then follow the right-hand hedge rounding a small shed and passing right of the bungalow. Where the hedge turns right, follow it then at the far end of the field turn left keeping left of a hedge and following it to the next corner of the field where you go straight on out to the road at Wigginton Heath.

Turn left onto this road and follow it for nearly half a mile passing Lodge Farm. At the far end of the farm, where there are fine views ahead towards distant hills in Warwickshire, opposite a drive turn left over a stile onto path HN21 bearing half right across a field to an oak tree then continuing to a stile in the far hedge. (If this stile is still missing, turn left and follow the hedge downhill to cross some rails in the bottom corner of the field.) Cross this stile and bear half left across the next field to an old iron gate in its bottom hedge. Climb through this with a fine view across Hook Norton opening out ahead then bear half right across the field to its bottom right-hand corner. Here go straight on through the hedge (if obstructed, use the hedge gap

100 yards to your left). Now bear half right across the next field heading for a gate and stile by an electricity pole in the second hedge ahead to cross a fence and descend a steep bank (the face of a disused ironstone quarry). At the bottom cross a ditch, a field and a fence then go through the gate by the electricity pole and turn left beside a left-hand hedge. Where the hedge bears slightly left, bear slightly right across the field corner to a hedge gap and culvert then go straight on to cross some rails in the next hedge. Now go straight on to cross some iron railings just right of a hedge corner and follow the left-hand hedge to a gate. Go through this then turn right over some rails and follow a fenced path down a slope into a field. Here turn sharp left onto path HN19 crossing a corner of the field to go through a gap in a thick hedge then keep straight on to cross a stile in the right hand hedge just beyond the last ash tree to enter a green lane. Turn left along this lane to cross a stile by a gate and a residential road then take a worn path straight on across an area of verge to reach a village street called East End. Turn right onto this and follow its winding course for nearly half a mile, later as Chapel Street, to reach the 'Bell Inn'.

WALK 17

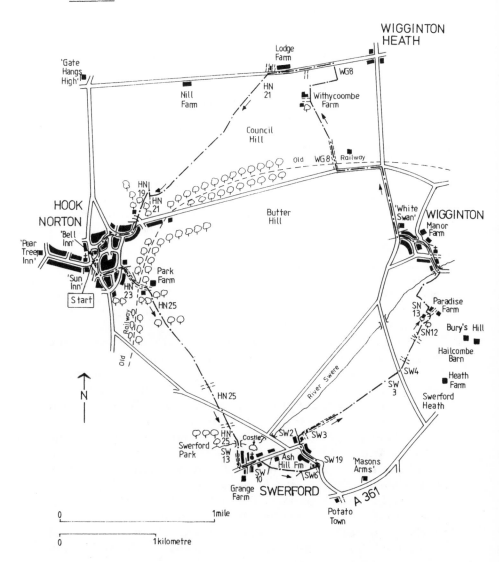

WALK 18 :   GREAT TEW

Length of Walk:	(A) 5.6 miles / 9.1 Km
	(B) 3.9 miles / 6.2 Km
Starting Point:	Road junction by the entrance to Great Tew
	village car park.
Grid Ref:	SP395293
Maps:	OS Landranger Sheets 151 & 164
	OS Pathfinder Sheets 1045 (SP43/53),
	1068 (SP22/32) & 1069 (SP42/52)

How to get there / Parking: Great Tew, 5 miles east of Chipping Norton, may be reached from the town by taking the A361 towards Banbury for 3 miles, then forking right onto a road signposted to 'The Tews'. At a fork go straight on, then at a T-junction turn left onto the B4022. After half a mile take the first turning right towards Great Tew where there is a public car park on your left.

Great Tew, with its thatched ironstone cottages and colourful gardens on a leafy hillside, has been described with some justification as one of the most picturesque villages in the Cotswolds. Much of the credit for its beauty must go to the landscape gardener John Claudius Loudon, who in 1808 not only completely redesigned the Estate laying out new farm roads following the contours, (some of which are followed during the course of the walks), but also planted large numbers of evergreen and exotic trees and shrubs, many of which still survive to beautify the area today. The attractive fifteenth-century village pub, the 'Falkland Arms', which was flying the Falkland Islands flag when the walk was in preparation, is named after the seventeenth-century Lord Falkland, Lucius Cary, who entertained such notable guests as Abraham Cowley, Edmund Waller and Ben Jonson at Great Tew Park before the Civil War and his early death at the Battle of Newbury in 1643. His house was, however, demolished and replaced by the present manor house early in the nineteenth century, while the nearby church, which is of Norman origin, was substantially altered in the fourteenth century. The village, which until recently all belonged to the Estate, was in a ruinous condition in the late 1970s but has thankfully now been restored to its former glory.

Both walks explore the beautiful valley to the north and east of Great Tew, part of which still bears the imprint of Loudon's landscaping, while Walk A also takes you over Iron Down with its superb views across the Swere valley towards Bloxham and Banbury.

Both walks start from the road junction by the entrance to Great Tew's village car park and take the side road into the village. At a T-junction by the post office turn right, then just past the 'Falkland Arms' turn left onto bridleway GT10 and take this rough lane straight on out of the village disregarding a branching lane to your left. On reaching a gate into a field, take a grassy track beside the Great Tew Park wall straight on through three fields with fine views across the valley to your left. By the far end of the park go straight on through a hedge gap, then ignore a hedge gap to your left and bear half left onto path SM14 following a left-hand hedge. At a corner of the field go straight on through a hedge gap then bear slightly right across the next field heading right of a lightning-damaged oak tree in the field beyond to pass through a hedge gap. Now continue to a hunting gate and bridge in an obvious gap in the middle of the next hedge. Having crossed the bridge, bear slightly left across a large field to cross a rail stile about 100 yards right of its far left-hand corner, then continue across a further field to a white gate in its far left-hand corner near the hamlet of Nether Worton (see Walk 13).

Do NOT go through this gate but turn sharp left onto bridleway SM17, a grassy track following a right-hand hedge. At the far end of the field go through a white gate then turn right through a hedge gap onto path SM16. Here bear half left across the field to cross a stream some 70 yards right of its far left-hand corner. (If there is still no bridge here, turn left to use the bridge on bridleway SM17 at the corner of the field, then go straight across the next field heading for the left side of the copse on Raven Hill until you reach a crossing grassy track.) Otherwise, having crossed the stream, bear slightly left across the next field heading for the left side of the copse on Raven Hill and passing just left of an oak tree to reach a crossing grassy track.

Walk B turns left onto this track (bridleway SM18) and follows it passing left of an oak tree to reach a gate. Go through this and take the track straight on beside a right-hand hedge. Eventually you enter a green lane known as Groveash Lane and follow its winding course for half a mile passing through a copse and becoming bridleway GT19. On reaching a T-junction with a farm road (bridleway GT18), turn left onto it rejoining Walk A. Now read the last paragraph.

Walk A crosses the grassy track rejoining bridleway SM17 and taking it straight on over a culvert by the corner of a fence and through a gate then up a terraced grassy track into the copse. Now follow a wide green lane straight on along the edge of the copse. On entering a field, follow the left-hand hedge to a gate right of a long shed at Upper Grove Ash Farm where there is a large artificial lake to your left. Go through this gate and take a grassy track beside a right-hand hedge straight on uphill past the buildings, gradually bearing left to pass through another gate. Here go straight on across the next field to a gate onto the farm drive, then take this drive straight on uphill with fine views to your left towards Ledwell and Great Tew Park, eventually bearing right and climbing to reach the B4031 near the top of Iron Down.

Turn left onto this road, then just before a left-hand bend turn right through a gate onto bridleway SN5a, a green lane leading you over the top of Iron Down. Where the lane ends, follow a right-hand hedge straight on downhill to a gate where panoramic views open out across the Swere valley towards Wigginton Heath ahead and Bloxham with its prominent spire and distant Banbury to your right. Now bear slightly left downhill to a gate in the bottom hedge then go straight on across the next field to the corner of a hedge. Here turn left and follow the right-hand hedge ignoring a gate in it. At the corner of the field go straight on through a gate then turn right and follow a right-hand hedge. By the second oak tree in the hedge turn sharp left onto bridleway SN5 passing left of a copse to reach a gate in the top corner of the field. Go through this and bear slightly right passing the corner of a left-hand fence then gradually diverging from the fence to reach a wide gap in the hedge ahead. Here go straight on to the corner of a fence by a barn at Hill Farm then follow the fence past the barn and bear half left across a field to a gate by the gable end of a bungalow. Go through this then turn right onto the farm drive and follow it straight on to the B4031. Cross this road and take bridleway GT17, a

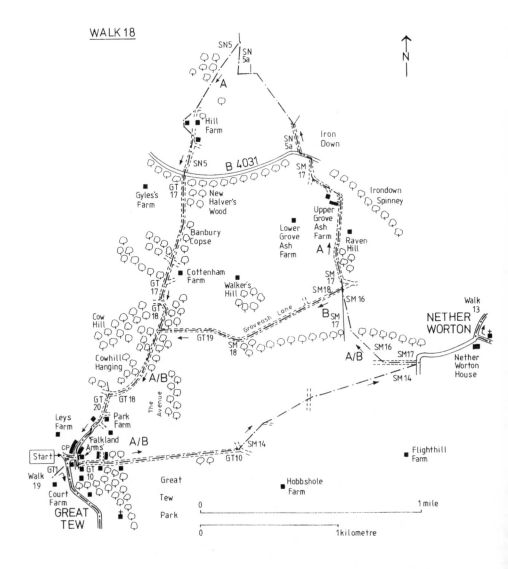

WALK 18

N

SN5 SN 5a

A

Hill Farm

SN 5a Iron Down

SN5 B 4031

SM 17

Gyles's Farm GT 17

New Halver's Wood

Irondown Spinney

Banbury Copse

Lower Grove Ash Farm

Upper Grove Ash Farm

A

Raven Hill

GT 17 Cottenham Farm

Walker's Hill

SM 17
SM18

Cow Hill

GT 18

Groveash Lane

B SM 17

SM 16

Walk 13

NETHER WORTON

Cowhill Hanging

GT 19

SM 18

A/B

SM16

SM17

Nether Worton House

A/B

The Avenue

SM 14

GT 20 GT 18

Leys Farm

Park Farm

Falkland Arms

A/B

CP

Start

Walk 19

GT

Court Farm

GREAT TEW

GT 10

SM 14

GT10

Flighthill Farm

Great

Tew

Park

Hobbshole Farm

0   1 mile

0   1 kilometre

LEDWELL

macadam farm road, straight on downhill for half a mile. Where the macadam road turns left, leave it and take a stony lane straight on. At a junction of lanes bear left onto bridleway GT18, which bears right to resume your previous direction and after some 200 yards rejoins **Walk B** at a track junction.

Now **Walks A and B** follow this stony lane straight on for a further 700 yards rounding the bottom of Cow Hill. Where the lane forks, turn left onto bridleway GT20 and follow this stony lane to the end of a village street at Great Tew by an attractive thatched cottage. Bear right onto this street and follow it uphill, soon passing more thatched cottages, then by the post office turn right for your starting point.

WALK 19 : CHURCH ENSTONE

Length of Walk:	(A)	9.4 miles / 15.1 Km
	(B)	7.8 miles / 12.5 Km
	(C)	3.7 miles / 5.9 Km
Starting Points:	(A/B)	Lychgate of St. Kenelm's Church, Church Enstone.
	(C)	Road junction by the entrance to Great Tew village car park.
Grid Refs:	(A/B) SP379251 / (C) SP395293
Maps:	OS Landranger Sheet 164
	OS Pathfinder Sheets 1068 (SP22/32) (all) & 1069 (SP42/52) (A/B only)

How to get there / Parking: (A/B) Church Enstone, 4.3 miles east of Chipping Norton, may be reached from the town by taking the A44 towards Oxford to the edge of Enstone. Here fork left onto the B4030 towards Bicester and follow its winding course for half a mile then turn left into a narrow road signposted to the 'Crown Inn'. By the pub bear right and look for a suitable parking space. If in difficulty, rejoin the B4030 and turn left into the Little Tew road where ample parking space is available.
(C) See Walk 18.

Notes: Parts of all three walks may be swampy after wet weather.

The twin villages of Church and Neat Enstone on either side of the Glyme valley with their fine stone-built houses and mediaeval tithe barn appear once to have been quite rich. This may have resulted partly from the fact that they are ranged around a triangle of ancient turnpike roads (the modern A44, B4022 and B4030) and in consequence, could once boast six coaching inns and partly from the seventeenth-century royal pleasure garden known as Queen Henrietta's Waterworks situated in the Glyme valley between the two villages. By 1800, however, the latter had become neglected, while the coming of the railways, which avoided hilly areas such as Enstone, led to the decline in importance of the turnpike roads and closure of three of the inns. Today some fine stone buildings,

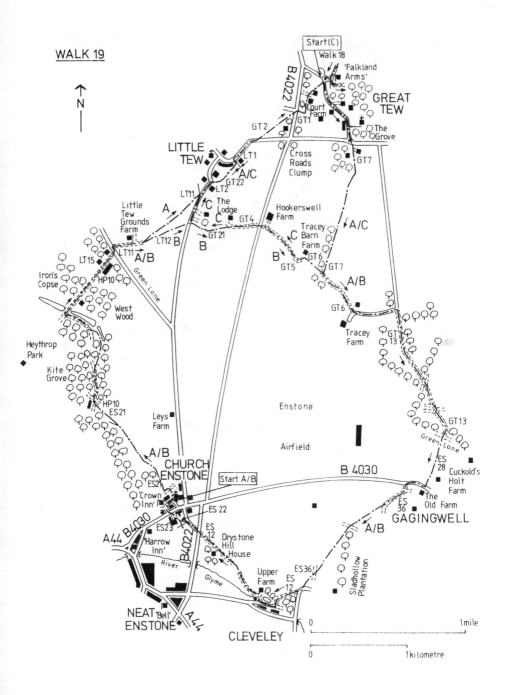

WALK 19

N

Start(C)
Walk 18
'Falkland Arms'
GREAT TEW
B 4022
Court Farm
GT1
GT 2
The Grove
LITTLE TEW
LT1
GT 22
A/C
Cross Roads Clump
GT 7
LT11
LT2
C
The Lodge
A
C
GT 4
Hookerswell Farm
A/C
Little Tew Grounds Farm
C
GT 21
Tracey Barn Farm
C
LT12
B
B
GT 6
LT11
A/B
GT5
GT 7
LT15
HP10
A/B
Iron's Copse
GT 6
West Wood
Green Lane
Tracey Farm
GT 13
Heythrop Park
Kite Grove
HP10
ES21
Leys Farm
Enstone
Airfield
GT13
Green Lane
A/B
CHURCH ENSTONE
Start A/B
B 4030
ES 28
Cuckold's Holt Farm
ES2
'Crown Inn'
ES 22
ES 36
The Old Farm
A/B
GAGINGWELL
ES23
ES 12
Drystone Hill House
A44 B4030
'Harrow Inn'
River
Glyme
Upper Farm
ES 12
ES36
Sladhollow Plantation
NEAT ENSTONE
'Bell'
A44
CLEVELEY

0   1mile

0   1kilometre

110

including the fourteenth-century cruck tithe barn, survive as does St. Kenelm's Church, originally a Saxon building (as suggested by its dedication to a Saxon saint) but rebuilt by the Normans and with a tower added in the fifteenth century.

All three walks explore the gently rolling Cotswold landscape to the north of the Glyme valley with Walks A and B passing through Heythrop Park with its pleasant woods and attractive lakes and visiting the picturesque sleepy hamlet of Cleveley, while Walks A and C visit both Great and Little Tew and sample the results of John Claudius Loudon's genial landscaping (see Walk 18).

Walks A and B start by the lychgate of St. Kenelm's Church, Church Enstone and take fenced path ES21 passing left of the lychgate, the church and the churchyard, then ignore a branching path to the right and continue to a small gate leading into a paddock. Go straight on beside a right-hand fence through the paddock then over a stile, a track and a second stile to enter a field. Now turn left and follow the left-hand fence to a corner of the field then turn right and follow a left-hand hedge downhill to the bottom corner. Here go straight on through a hedge gap and uphill to a small gate at the corner of a hedge, then keep straight on, heading between the far end of the belt of trees to your left and an oak tree, with Heythrop Park house just visible through the treetops ahead, to pass through a gap in the far hedge. Now go straight on towards a clump of trees ahead crossing a dip and ignoring a handgate to your left, then passing left of two sycamores to reach stepping stones across a stream and a stile into Heythrop Park.

Cross these and take path HP10 bearing slightly right, passing right of a clump of trees and aiming for a wooden electricity pylon. Now follow the powerline through a gap in the trees to the end of a macadam drive where you turn right through a hedge gap into a wood called Kite Grove, then turn left onto a grassy track. Where the track forks, turn right and follow a track through the woods for some 300 yards. At another fork bear slightly right onto a signposted path descending gently to pass a thatched hut and join the banks of the stream. Eventually, near a dam retaining a lake, you climb to join a stony track onto which you bear slightly right. On reaching a macadam estate road, turn right onto it (still on path HP10) crossing a bridge and continuing uphill for half a mile, soon with a view of

Heythrop Park house behind you. Designed by Sir John Vanbrugh, architect of Blenheim Palace, for Charles Talbot, Earl of Shrewsbury, in the early eighteenth century, Heythrop Park was destroyed by fire in 1831 and rebuilt in similar style by the railway contractor Thomas Brassey in 1870. At one time owned by the Jesuits, Heythrop Park now houses a staff college of the National Westminster Bank.

Having passed through the headquarters of a circus, the road (now path LT15) reaches a public road called Green Lane. Turn left onto this, then after some 80 yards turn right onto path LT11, the drive to Little Tew Grounds Farm. At the farm take a fenced grassy track straight on to pass through the left-hand of two gates into a field. Here **Walk A** bears slightly left across the field passing the end of a fenced stream and heading towards a radio station on the skyline to reach a stile and footbridge right of a row of trees in the bottom hedge. Cross these and a barbed-wire fence, then go straight on uphill to a gate. Here keep straight on to a concealed gap in the right-hand hedge leading to a road onto which you turn left joining Walk C. Now omit the next paragraph.

Walk B takes path LT12 straight on across the field to a gate in the far corner. Here cross a road and go through a hedge gap opposite onto path GT21 following a concealed left-hand stream through two fields. By a ruined cottage join its grassy drive (path GT4) and continue along it to a gate onto the B4022. Here take path GT5, a farm track, straight on through three fields ignoring a branching track to the left towards Hookerswell Farm. Near the far end of the third field turn left over a culvert and through gates then cross a field to gates right of the ruins of Tracey Barn Farm. Go through the gates and take path GT6 following a right-hand hedge along the bottom of a field, then take a grassy track straight on through a copse into another field where you rejoin Walk A and go straight on. Now omit the next three paragraphs.

Walks A and C follow the road to a left-hand bend on the edge of Little Tew, an attractive Cotswold village with a church with an unusual saddleback tower built by George Street in 1835. At this bend turn right onto path LT2 between a Dutch barn and a low stone-built shed then pass through a former gateway and go straight downhill across a field to a clump of trees in the valley bottom. Here cross a small stream and a wooden fence then take path GT22 following a left-hand hedge uphill. Where the hedge gives way to a stone wall, turn left over a stile onto enclosed paved path LT1 and follow it to a stone stile onto a village street at Little Tew.

Turn right onto this road and follow it uphill out of the village rounding a sharp right-hand bend. About 40 yards short of a large beech tree turn left through a hedge gap onto path GT2. Now bear half right across the field heading for the middle of a copse on the skyline and passing left of a fenced radio station to reach a rail stile leading to a road junction. Here cross the B4022 and take path GT1 through a kissing-gate opposite. Follow the right-hand hedge towards a tall chimney, then, where the overhead wires turn left, do likewise joining a left-hand hedge and following it to a gate into a farmyard at Court Farm. Here go straight on to meet the farm drive then turn right onto it and immediately left over a stile to follow a right-hand hedge. Where the hedge turns right, leave it and bear slightly right across the field with fine views towards Great Tew ahead to reach a kissing-gate onto the village street, onto which **Walk C** turns left for the car park while **Walk A** turns right. (See Walk 18 for historical details.)

Walk C starts from the road junction by the entrance to Great Tew village car park and takes the priority road uphill joining **Walk A.** **Walks A and C** now follow the left-hand roadside footway uphill with Great Tew Park soon coming into view to your left. Shortly afterwards the footway transfers to the other side of the road and ends opposite the path to the church. Here go straight on to reach a road junction where you fork left then cross the major road and take path GT7 straight on along a cottage drive. By its garage fork right through a gate into a field then follow a right-hand stone wall straight on to a hedge gap at the far end of the field. Now follow a right-hand hedge generally straight on through two more fields. At the far end of the second field cross some rails then **Walk A** turns left onto path GT6 omitting the next paragraph.

Walk C turns right onto path GT6 passing through a copse then following a left-hand hedge to go through gates by the ruins of Tracey Barn Farm. Now take path GT5 bearing left across a field to pass through more gates, then turn right and take a grassy track through three fields to the B4022. Cross this, take path GT4 through a gate opposite and follow a grassy track straight on. Where the track turns right towards a ruined cottage, leave it and take path GT21 following the right-hand stream straight on through two fields to reach another road. Turn right onto this and follow it to the top of a hill where you rejoin Walk A. Now go back four paragraphs.

Walks A and B now take path GT6 following a grassy track beside a left-hand hedge through three fields, in the third field bearing slightly right across it to a gate onto a road near a cottage. Turn left onto this road and follow it for over a quarter mile. At a sharp left-hand bend turn right into a stony lane and follow it downhill to a ford and footbridge then take bridleway GT13 straight on for over half a mile ignoring branching tracks to your right then your left and eventually reaching a concrete road. Turn left onto this, then, after some 40 yards, turn right then left onto a concrete road crossing a field and passing through a tree belt to enter an old green lane. Here turn right following the concrete surface, then after about 30 yards turn left through a bridlegate onto bridleway ES28 following a left-hand fence to the far side of the field. Now bear slightly right passing through a hedge gap right of a gate and following a left-hand hedge through two fields to a gate onto the B4030 at Gagingwell opposite The Old Farm.

Turn right onto this busy road rounding a blind left-hand bend, then by ornamental gateposts turn left through steel gates onto bridleway ES36, a concrete farm track. After about 50 yards ignore a branching track to your left then bear right. Where the track later bears left, leave it and go straight on across the field to a hedge gap just right of its far corner. Go through this and bear half left across the next field to a hedge gap by the right-hand end of a tree belt. Here disregard a crossing bridleway and go straight on through the gap crossing the next field diagonally to pass just left of the second wooden electricity pylon. Now keep straight on ignoring a crossing grass track and reaching a hedge gap in the far corner of the field leading to a bend in a road. Do not join the road but turn right onto bridleway ES12, a sunken green lane, descending gently to cross a footbridge over the River Glyme by a ford. Now turn right into a green lane which follows the river to the end of a village street in Cleveley.

Take this road straight on, then, where it forks, bear right onto bridleway ES12 crossing a bridge over the river and passing a large attractive duckpond. Now bear half left into a green lane which climbs at first then levels out. On emerging over a bridge into a field, follow a left-hand fence straight on uphill, soon entering another green lane and following it to the B4022. Cross this and take a narrow road called Cling-Clang Lane straight on downhill and up again. After passing under a power line, turn left over a stile by a gate and take path ES22 bearing half right and following a right-hand fence and stone wall with a fine view to your left across the Glyme valley towards Neat Enstone. On reaching a stile, turn right over it onto fenced path ES23 and follow it to another stile. Here turn right onto a stone drive, soon turning right again onto a rough macadam road leading to the B4030 opposite a small green. Cross the main road and take a macadam path across the green to join a side road near the 'Crown Inn', then bear right for your starting point.

WALK 20 : CHIPPING NORTON

Length of Walk: 8.8 miles / 14.1 Km
Starting Point: Chipping Norton Town Hall.
Grid Ref: SP313271
Maps: OS Landranger Sheets 163 & 164
OS Pathfinder Sheet 1068 (SP22/32)
Parking: A public car park off the A44 (Stow-on-the-Wold road) is signposted from its junction with the A361 by the Town Hall.

Chipping Norton, built largely of Pudlicote stone on the side of a high Cotswold ridge, would, at first sight, seem a strange location for a town, but being at the crossroads of the ancient London–Worcester road (A44) and the A361 Banbury–Swindon road and near the old Oxford–Birmingham turnpike (now the A3400), it has never been remote. Indeed in the Middle Ages, when the wool trade made the Cotswolds rich, Chipping Norton with its market (from which the first part of its name derives) must have been a prosperous centre for trading and weaving, as can be seen from its beautiful church rebuilt in the fourteenth and fifteenth centuries. Apart from the church, the town, locally known as 'Chippy', can boast some fine seventeenth- and eighteenth-century houses and inns, a row of almshouses built in 1640 and an imposing nineteenth-century classical town hall which dominates the town centre. When approaching the town from the west, however, its most striking feature is Bliss Mill with its tall chimney, a former tweed mill built in 1872 and a splendid example of Victorian industrial design.

The walk, which offers a whole series of superb views across the Cotswolds, soon leaves Chipping Norton behind and crosses a lofty ridge into the Sars Brook valley before climbing to the fascinating hilltop village of Churchill. You then follow an attractive section of the D'Arcy Dalton Way by way of the estate village of Cornwell to Salford before returning over a hill into Chipping Norton.

Starting from the junction of the A44 and A361 by Chipping Norton Town Hall, take the A361 towards Burford. At a mini-roundabout by the 'Kings Arms Hotel' turn left, then at a second mini-roundabout bear right (still on the A361). Now at a left-hand bend turn right into Walterbush Road and follow it for nearly half a mile to its far end. Here take path CN1 straight on into a field then continue across the field parallel to a left-hand powerline, with wide views opening out across the hills towards the Gloucestershire town of Stow-on-the-Wold on a hilltop ahead and towards Bliss Mill in the valley to your right. Go through a gap at a junction of hedges and bear half left across a large field heading just left of a single tree and a clump of trees to reach a hedge gap onto a road.

Cross this road then take path CH12 straight on through a gap in a stone wall, over a wire fence and across the corner of a field aiming for the second telegraph pole along the drive to Sarsgrove Farm. Turn left onto this drive and follow it to the far end of the field. Where the drive turns left, leave it and bear slightly right across a field, heading towards Parsonage Farm on the other side of the valley, with a view of Churchill with its prominent church tower on a rise to your right. On reaching a stone wall, pass through a gate in it then go straight on across two fields aiming for the bottom right-hand corner of Sarsgrove Wood in the valley bottom and passing through a hedge gap to join the outside edge of a right-hand copse at the far corner of the second field. Follow the edge of the copse downhill to a culvert and gate in the valley bottom. Go through the gate and take path SR7 straight on uphill towards the barn of Parsonage Farm. By the corner of a wooden fence bear half right to pass right of the farmhouse then follow a left-hand stone wall to a gate at the far end of the field. Go through this and keep straight on across parkland to cross a wooden fence left of a tall ash tree then continue across a paddock, passing Sarsden Glebe to your left, to cross a wooden fence in the far corner. Now bear half left and follow an alternating left-hand hedge and ha-ha. Where the ha-ha bears away left, leave it and go straight on across the field and a dip to pass through a gate. Here turn right across a corner of the next field to cross a culvert left of a stone shed. Now go through a handgate and take path CH12 bearing half left across a field with pronounced ridge and furrows denoting mediaeval cultivation to cross a rail stile in the far corner. Turn right onto a path along a bank above a road dropping to join the road (and the D'Arcy

117

Dalton Way) and following it uphill into Churchill.

Churchill, once a market town, has a church familiar to walkers from Oxford as its tower is a scaled-down model of Magdalen College tower, while its walls and ceiling are based on New College and Christ Church Hall respectively. Built in 1826 to replace a thirteenth-century building at the bottom end of the village of which only the chancel remains, it was designed by Squire John Haughton Langston, in whose memory the nearby ornate conduit was installed in 1863. In the eighteenth century the village was the birthplace of two famous men: Warren Hastings (1732–1818), first Governor General of India, and William Smith (1769–1839), a canal-builder who in 1815 published the first geological map of England and Wales and is known as the 'father of British geology'. A stone memorial to him stands on a small green in the centre of the village.

At a road junction by the 'new' church turn left onto the B4450 and follow it for about 150 yards. At a left-hand bend turn right onto path CH1, a gravel lane, and follow it to a stile into a field where a fine view opens out across the Evenlode valley towards Stow-on-the-Wold. Now bear half right across the field towards a large stone cottage with two rear gables, crossing four stiles to reach a gate and stile which lead in 70 yards to Kingham Road. Cross this road and continue along a macadamed alleyway then a gravel drive to a road called Hastings Hill leading down to the old church. Turn left onto this then, after some 70 yards, turn right over a stile by a gate onto path CH6. On entering a field, bear half left across it crossing a stile in a wooden fence and continuing across a second field to a stile into a tree-belt. Go straight on through the tree-belt crossing a stream and later another stile then bear slightly left across a field to a hedge gap right of three trees in a corner. Now bear slightly right heading towards a copse on the skyline to reach a gap in the next hedge. Here cross a footbridge then bear half left across a corner of the next field to a hedge gap and footbridge leading to the old Chipping Norton Branch Line, opened in 1855 and closed in 1962.

Cross the old railway and descend a bank to a stile then bear half right across a field to cross a footbridge over a wide stream. Now bear half right across the next field to cross a footbridge in its far corner then take path KH10 following a right-hand hedge to a hedge gap and culvert leading to bridleway KH11. Cross this bridleway and some wooden rails opposite then take path KH9 bearing half right across a field to a gate in its right-hand hedge. Do NOT go through this gate but turn left onto a grassy track and follow it uphill beside the right-hand hedge to double gates. Go through these and take a macadamed farm road straight on, soon bearing right to reach Kingham Hill Farm. Where the road forks, take the right-hand option straight on with its surface changing to concrete and eventually ending. Here go straight on through double gates and across a field to a gate then continue across a second field to cross a stile and footbridge. Now take path CO7 bearing slightly left across a field to a gate between oak trees then bear slightly left again, climbing to cross a stile in the top left-hand corner of the field. Here go straight on across parkland passing just right of a large tree-stump and continuing to a stile onto a road about 30 yards left of some ornamental gates from which there is a good view of the façade of Cornwell's Georgian manor house.

Cross the stile and descend steps to the road then turn left onto it. Ignore a private road to your right into Cornwell village, to which the owner of the Estate has prevented public access, then turn right onto the Moreton-in-Marsh road and follow it downhill and up again. By the far end of the village at a sharp left-hand bend turn right onto path CO1, a macadam drive. Where the drive begins to turn left, leave it and take path CO2 straight on past the right-hand end of a hedge into an orchard then bear half left across the orchard to a hedge gap in its far corner where there is a clear view of Chipping Norton ahead. Here cross a wooden fence and bear half right across parkland passing left of a clump of trees and Cornwell's tiny Norman church then dropping to cross a gated culvert in the valley bottom. Now go straight on uphill to a gate and kissing-gate where you turn right onto a narrow road.

After about 30 yards, turn left onto bridleway CO4, the drive to Glebe Farm. Where the drive forks, keep right. On reaching the farm buildings, bear slightly right between them then at the far side of the farm wiggle left then right onto a track which enters a field and follows its left-hand hedge with a fine view towards Chipping Norton to your right. At the far side of the field take the track (now bridleway SA10) through the central of three hedge gaps then bearing slightly right to follow a right-hand hedge with a view ahead of Salford church, rebuilt in the late Middle Ages but retaining some Norman features. Now follow the track's winding course for a further half-mile to a gate onto the A44. Cross this busy road carefully and turn right along its wide verge, soon leaving the D'Arcy Dalton Way.

At Salford Turn turn left onto a road into this stone-built village then fork immediately right into Lower End ignoring branching roads to right and left and passing the 'Black Horse'. Where the road turns sharp left, leave it and take path SA9 straight on along a macadam drive into Village Farm. Where its surface ends, go straight on through a gate and bear slightly left onto a fenced track. Take this straight on for half a mile to the top of a hill where there is a fine view of Salford in the valley behind. Now go though a hedge gap, cross a stile left of a hedge ahead and take path CN20 beside the hedge to a stile at the far end of the field. Here go straight on across the next field, later heading for a bush left of a line of trees ahead to cross a stile by this bush. Now follow a right-hand hedge straight on downhill to cross two stiles at the bottom end of the field then leave the hedge and go straight on, passing left of one clump of bushes and right of a second to reach a stile by a gate. Cross this, a farm road and a second stile by a gate then go straight on downhill past the corner of a wood to a footbridge in the valley bottom. Now take worn path CN18 straight on uphill to a kissing-gate into a recreation ground. Go through this and take path CN17 straight on, passing just left of several pieces of play equipment with a view of Chipping Norton church to your left, to reach a kissing-gate in a corner onto the A44. Turn left onto this road and follow it uphill to your starting point.

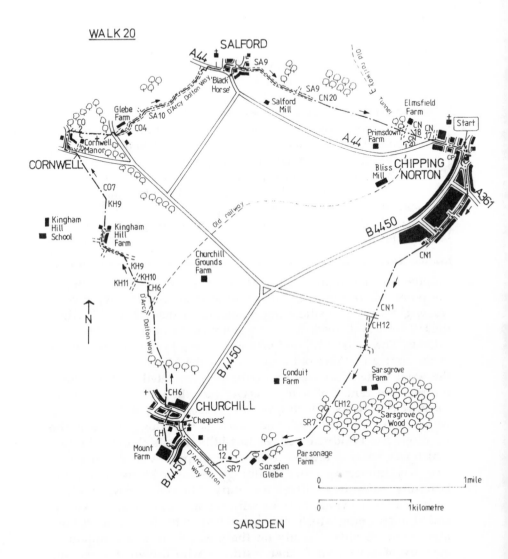

WALK 20

SALFORD

SA9

SA9

CN20

Black Horse

D'Arcy Dalton Way

Glebe Farm

SA10

CO

CO4

Cornwell Manor

CORNWELL

CO7

KH9

Kingham Hill School

Kingham Hill Farm

KH9

KH10

KH11

CH6

D'Arcy Dalton Way

Churchill Grounds Farm

Old railway

Salford Mill

Primsdown Farm

Bliss Mill

Elmsfield Farm

CN 18

CN 17

Start

CHIPPING NORTON

CP

A44

A361

B4450

CN1

CN1

CH12

Sarsgrove Farm

Sarsgrove Wood

CH6

CHURCHILL

'Chequers'

CH 1

Mount Farm

CH 12

SR7

D'Arcy Dalton Way

B4450

Conduit Farm

CH12

SR7

Parsonage Farm

Sarsden Glebe

B4450

↑ N —

0   1mile

0   1kilometre

SARSDEN

121

WALK 21 : SHIPTON-UNDER-WYCHWOOD

Length of Walk: 8.0 miles / 12.9 Km

Starting Point: Shipton-under-Wychwood Church.

Grid Ref: SP280180

Maps: OS Landranger Sheet 163
OS Pathfinder Sheets 1068 (SP22/32)
& 1091 (SP21/31)

How to get there / Parking: Shipton-under-Wychwood, some
6 miles southwest of Chipping Norton, may be reached from
the town by taking the A361 towards Burford. In the village,
after rounding a left-hand bend by the 'Red Horse', continue
for 300 yards to a right-hand bend by a walled green, then
opposite the 'Shaven Crown' turn sharp left into Church
Street and find a suitable parking place.

Notes: Severe mud may be encountered in places, particularly
on bridleway FI10, even in dry weather.

Shipton-under-Wychwood, a large village in the Evenlode valley at
the point where the river turns northeast around the Wychwood
ridge, gives the immediate impression of mediaeval wealth when
the tall spire of its twelfth-century church comes into view from the
hillside. The name 'Shipton' meaning 'sheep farm', indeed, points
to the source of Cotswold prosperity in the Middle Ages, namely
the wool trade. This was no doubt supplemented by the village
forming the centre of a royal estate including the ancient royal
forest of Wychwood which gives it the second part of its name and
which until the 1850s covered much of the ridge between the
Evenlode and Windrush valleys. In addition to its church, Shipton,
which was home to the fourteenth-century poet William Langland,
also has numerous other buildings of interest including the
tastefully renovated fifteenth-century 'Shaven Crown', which
derives its name from its links with the monks of Bruern Abbey,
and Shipton Court, which was remodelled by the Laceys in 1603 but
may be much older. Finally on the green there is a fountain in
memory of seventeen former residents who drowned when the
'Cospatrick', which was taking them to a new life in New Zealand,
caught fire and sank off Tristan de Cunha in 1874.

The walk, which offers a series of superb views of the Evenlode valley and surrounding hills, takes you by way of Milton-under-Wychwood to the remote Cotswold hill villages of Fifield and Idbury before returning through the woods around the riverside hamlet of Bruern to Shipton-under-Wychwood.

Starting from the entrance to Shipton-under-Wychwood Church, take Church Street back past the green to the A361 opposite the 'Shaven Crown'. Turn left onto the A361 and follow it for over a third of a mile passing attractive stone cottages with mullioned windows as well as Shipton Court and Shipton Grange. After rounding a sharp right-hand bend by the 'Lamb Inn', at a sharp left-hand bend by the entrance to 'Tall Trees' leave the main road and take path SU12 straight on along the tree-lined Dog Kennel Lane for nearly half a mile with its walls and trees later giving way to hedges. Where the lane ends at the top of the second rise and views open out ahead towards Milton-under-Wychwood and Fifield beyond, bear half right through a kissing-gate and take a fenced path downhill to cross a concealed footbridge and stile right of a gate. Now take path MW5 bearing half right towards the left-hand end of the houses at Milton-under-Wychwood and crossing two fields to reach gates leading to a bend in a village street.

Take Jubilee Lane straight on to reach High Street then turn right. After some 30 yards, just past the Baptist church to your right, turn left onto bridleway MW2, a lane between cottages leading to a field. Now take a grassy track beside a telephone line straight on across three fields to a gate then continue along a fenced track to the top of Little Hill. Here the track bears slightly left and becomes bridleway BR8. Now just past the third telephone pole bear half left off the fenced track over a stile onto path BR9, then bear half right across two fields to cross a stile, a footbridge and another stile. Now bear half left across the next field to a gate onto a road left of some cottages.

Cross this road and go through a gate opposite onto bridleway BR10 with fine views towards Idbury ahead and Fifield to your left, then bear half left across the field heading towards the right-hand end of Fifield to reach gates by a hollybush. Go through these and take bridleway BR11 following a left-hand hedge. Where the hedge wiggles slightly to the right, bear half right across the field to the bottom end of a wiggly hedge on the hillside ahead. Here go through a bridlegate and take path FI2 ignoring another bridlegate ahead and bearing half right to pass through a clump of five small lime trees left of Fifield House with its prominent slate roof and reach a gate into a lane at Fifield. Formerly known as Fifield Merrymouth after the fourteenth-century lord of the manor, John de Muremouth, this small village can boast a thirteenth-century church with an equally ancient spire and its former name is perpetuated by the 'Merrymouth Inn' on the A424 at the top of the ridge.

Before continuing, turn round to admire the fine view across the valley behind you towards Milton-under-Wychwood and the remaining area of Wychwood Forest beyond, then follow the lane to a road junction. Here go straight on, soon rounding a left-hand bend, then turn immediately right through a kissing-gate onto walled path FI9 to reach another kissing-gate where views open out towards Idbury ahead and the Evenlode valley to your right. Now follow a left-hand fence straight on across a dip to a gate and kissing-gate then keep straight on across a field with pronounced ridges and furrows from mediaeval cultivation to a concealed stile leading to a footbridge and stile. Cross these then climb some steps and continue uphill to a hedge gap and across the next field to a precarious footbridge over a ravine. Having crossed this, take path ID1 bearing slightly right across a field with pronounced ridges and furrows to cross a stile under an ash tree. Now follow a left-hand hedge with Idbury coming into view again to reach some gates. Cross a concealed stile to your right and take a worn path bearing slightly right across a field. At the bottom of a dip fork half right to reach a culvert in the far right-hand corner of the field. Cross this and admire a fine view back towards Fifield and the Evenlode valley then turn left over a stile onto path ID1a following a grassy drive then a macadam road uphill to a road junction in Idbury.

Tiny as it is, the hilltop village of Idbury is not without interest as its Tudor manor house is where J W Robertson Scott founded 'The Countryman' magazine in 1927 which is today still published in nearby Burford, while the Norman church which was altered and extended in the fifteenth century is where the renowned engineer Sir Benjamin Baker, builder of the Forth railway bridge, the first Aswan Dam and part of the London Underground, is buried.

Here turn right passing the church. At a left-hand bend turn right again through gates onto bridleway ID3 with panoramic views of the

Evenlode valley ahead and to your left and bear slightly left to pass through two more gates. Now bear half left following a grassy track beside a left-hand hedge through two fields then straight on across two more fields. On entering a fifth field, take bridleway FI13 bearing half right across it to a hedge gap by a corner of a wood known as Herbert's Heath. Go through this then bear half left and follow a grassy track along the outside edge of the wood to enter a green lane. Turn left into it joining bridleway FI10, then at a fork go straight on. Where the main track turns left, leave it and take a grassy track straight on through the wood for nearly half a mile ignoring a crossing track, crossing a stream where the track narrows to a muddy path and later passing fields to your right. On eventually reaching crossing bridleway FI14, turn left onto it, then immediately turn right onto path FI19. At a five-way junction take a grassy track straight on to a gate and stile visible ahead. Ignore the stile and go straight on through the gate into the left-hand field following a right-hand fence and belt of trees straight on across two fields on Fifield Heath with fine views ahead towards Churchill and Sarsden House in the second field to reach stiles flanking a farm road. Cross these and follow a right-hand hedge, later the edge of Cocksmoor Copse straight on, gradually bearing left to a stile leading onto the Oxfordshire Way. Turn right onto this then ignore a fork to your right and take bridleway FI16 straight on through the woods to a bridlegate into a field. Here take bridleway BR2 straight on along the outside edge of the wood to a bridlegate onto a road at Bruern.

Cross this road and take bridleway BR1 straight on through a bridlegate opposite bearing half left across parkland passing Bruern Abbey. Built by the Cope family on the site of a twelfth-century Cistercian abbey in the early eighteenth century, the present house was home to Sir John Cope, commander-in-chief of forces in Scotland at the time of the 1745 rebellion. Although his forces were routed by Bonny Prince Charlie at Prestonpans, Cope was not blamed for this defeat and the following year the rebellion was crushed at the Battle of Culloden.

On nearing the rear corner of the abbey garden, bear half right and follow a right-hand wooden fence to cross a stile by a gate then bear slightly left across a field to a bridlegate into Bruern Wood. In the wood take a wide fire-break straight on. At its far end ignore a crossing track and bear half left through a bridlegate into a field. Here take bridleway MW1 bearing slightly right and following a right-hand hedge, with fine views down the Evenlode valley, to a bridlegate into a fenced bridleway leading to Lyneham Road. Cross this road and take fenced bridleway MW1 straight on to a gate and stile. Now bear slightly right across the next field to a gate and stile where Shipton-under-Wychwood comes into view ahead. Continue across another field to a further gate and stile then take bridleway SU3 bearing slightly left and following a grassy track across the field, eventually bearing right and reaching the corner of a hedge. Here turn left and follow a right-hand hedge to a hedge gap into a green lane known as Meadow Lane. Turn right into this lane (now on bridleway SU2). After about 250 yards you cross a bridge and continue along a roadside pavement. Ignore three residential roads to your right then, where the right-hand stone wall ends, turn right through gates into a recreation ground and take path SU4 bearing half left across it to gates onto the A361. Go through these and turn right then immediately left crossing the road and taking Church Path (SU6), a macadam road which narrows to an alleyway and leads you across the churchyard to your starting point.

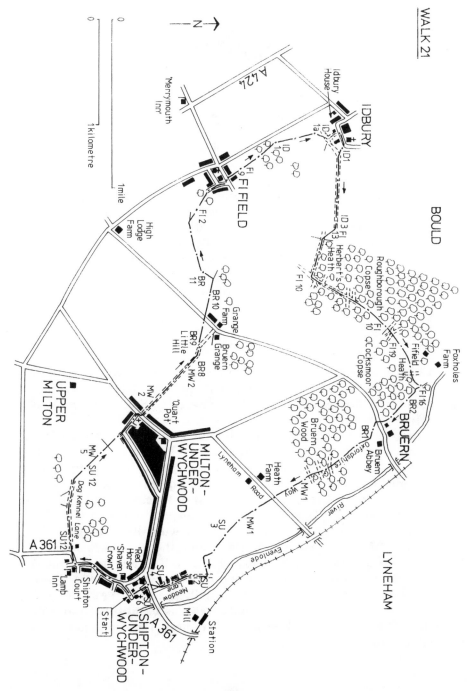

WALK 22 :   CHARLBURY

Length of Walk: (A) 10.1 miles / 16.3 Km
                        (B) 7.6 miles / 12.3 Km
Starting Point: Charlbury Station.
Grid Ref: SP352194
Maps: OS Landranger Sheet 164
             OS Pathfinder Sheets 1068 (SP22/32)
             & 1091 (SP21/31)

How to get there / Parking: Charlbury, 6 miles northwest of
    Woodstock, may be reached from the town by taking the
    A44 towards Chipping Norton and Evesham for 2 miles
    then turning left onto the B4437. On reaching the town,
    follow signs for Burford (no road numbers) until you reach
    the railway station where extensive parking is available.
    If full, return towards the town and find a suitable on-street
    parking space.

Charlbury, a small former market town on the slops of the Evenlode
valley, has an attractive centre with mainly eighteenth-century
stone-built houses and inns. Unlike neighbouring towns such as
Witney, it does not have wide spacious streets or fine civic
buildings and the Norman church with a thirteenth-century tower
drastically 'restored' in Victorian times is relatively modest. This
seems to be because Eynsham Abbey, which held the town up to the
Reformation, did not encourage its growth while Arthur Young
pointed out that the vast ancient Forest of Wychwood, to which it
was the gateway, yielded very little in financial terms. In Victorian
times, however, great changes occurred with the coming of the
Oxford–Worcester railway in 1853 and the disafforestation of
Wychwood in 1857 which led to much tree felling and the enormous
historic parish of Charlbury being dismembered with the 'forest
villages' becoming independent. The railway turned the town into a
focal point for the area and together with its beautiful countryside
made Charlbury into a popular dormitory for commuters into
Oxford and even London.

Both walks lead you from the town up the gentle slopes to the east to the Salt Track, an ancient green road once used for transporting salt from the Midlands. Walk A then explores Ditchley Park with its imposing house and abundant woodland before both walks continue through the picturesque village of Spelsbury and then turn south with superb views of the Evenlode valley to reach Charlbury.

Both walks start from the entrance to Charlbury Station and take the station approach out to the B4437. Turn right onto it crossing the River Evenlode then turn right into Church Lane. Where the road narrows, go straight on through gates into the churchyard and take a macadam path bearing left past the church to a bend in Church Street. Take this road straight on uphill to a T-junction by the 'Bull' then turn right into Market Street. Just past the 'Farmers' turn left into Fisher's Lane. At a T-junction turn right into Pooles Lane then just past Sandford Rise turn left through a gap onto path CB15 between a stone wall and a stream at first, then crossing a stile and continuing along an alleyway to the B4022/B4437.

Cross this road and turn right onto its pavement. Just past Blenheim Farm House turn immediately left onto path CB15 between cottages. Behind the cottages ignore a garden gate ahead and bear slightly right following a left-hand fence along the edge of a tree belt to cross one of two stiles by a gate. Now follow the valley bottom to a gate and stile into Blenheim Farm Nature Reserve. Continue through it to cross a stile in its far right-hand corner then climb some steps and take a fenced path past a plantation. At its far end ignore a kissing-gate to your left and bear slightly right onto a path along the middle of a narrow scrub belt. On entering a field, turn left and go through a hedge gap into a green lane (bridleway CB13). Take this lane straight on for a third of a mile past a large stone quarry to your left. On emerging onto a grassy track, turn left onto it, soon bearing right and later joining a left-hand hedge to reach Dustfield Farm. Here take the farm drive straight on, soon turning left onto an ancient green road called the Salt Track (SP31) and following it for over a third of a mile to Ditchley Road by twin lodges of Ditchley Park. Now keep straight on for a further 300 yards ignoring a branching track to your right into Model Farm. About 130 yards further on, **Walk A** turns right onto waymarked path SP36 into a plantation. Now omit the next paragraph.

Walk B takes the Salt Track (SP31) straight on for a further 700 yards to a house called Norman's Grove then continues along a macadam road for half a mile, soon leaving the Salt Track and rejoining Walk A, to reach a crossroads with the B4022. Now omit the next three paragraphs.

Walk A takes path SP36 soon leaving the plantation and following a grassy track straight on beside the plantation for a quarter mile. About 150 yards short of the far end of the field turn right onto a crossing farm track through the plantation. Where it turns right, turn left onto a fenced grassy track, soon passing between plantations to a gate into parkland. Here follow the left-hand fence straight on. Where it bears slightly left, leave it and bear slightly right across the park, crossing an avenue of trees with a side view of Ditchley House to your left and eventually reaching a gate and cattle grid on an estate drive by the near corner of a copse. Go through the gate left of the cattle grid then turn right through a second gate and take a wide fenced track beside the copse. At the far end of the copse turn left onto path ES61 passing just right of a tall tree to reach a corner of a fence where there is a fine view of the façade of Ditchley House to your left.

The present Ditchley House was built in 1722 by the Earl of Lichfield to a Classical design by James Gibbs, also architect of St. Martin's-in-the-Fields Church in London. Its beautiful interior with Italian stucco was designed by William Kent who also laid out the park. Today the house is a conference centre and has been used by the government as a location for secluded summitry.

Here bear slightly left onto path ES59, passing between a left-hand copse and a row of beech trees to reach a gate with a further good view of Ditchley House to your left. Now continue along an avenue of tall lime trees to an estate drive. Turn left onto this, keeping right at a fork. At a five-way junction, bear slightly left onto path ES60 to a cattle grid and gates. Here take path SP35 straight on along a stone track, ignoring branching tracks to your right then to your left and soon entering Dog Kennel Wood. After a quarter mile the track leaves the wood and follows its outside edge. Where it re-enters what is now Deadman's Riding Wood, leave it and take a grassy track straight on along the outside edge of the wood. On nearing the far corner of the field, follow the track into Laurel Wood. Here ignore a crossing track and go straight on through the wood with a cypress plantation to your left, disregarding a branching track to your left and reaching a corner of a field. Now turn left along the outside edge of Shilcott Wood with wide views to your left towards Enstone Airfield. At another corner of the field go straight on through a finger of woodland into another field with a fine view towards Spelsbury ahead. Here turn left bearing immediately right and following the edge of the wood for a third of a mile later bearing left to a hedge gap leading to the Salt Track (SP31). Turn left onto this then, after 50 yards, turn sharp right onto a macadam road rejoining Walk B and continuing for a third of a mile to a crossroads with the B4022.

Walks A and B now take the Taston road straight on for 250 yards. At the far end of the first field bear half left through a hedge gap onto path SP13 heading just right of Coathouse Farm with a view up the Evenlode valley ahead, to pass the corner of a hedge and continue to the far corner of the field. Here cross the farm drive and bear half right onto fenced bridleway SP10, ignoring a crossing path then descending through a spinney to a bridlegate and collapsed stone bridge in the valley bottom. Now go straight on up a field to gates in the far corner. Go through these and follow a right-hand hedge through further gates by a cottage and along a lane to a village street in Spelsbury.

Turn left onto this road to reach the B4026 then turn right taking care at a blind bend. By a stone fountain with a canopy erected in memory of Constantine Augustus Dillon (1813–1853) turn left into Church Lane towards the church with its massive Norman tower which once bore a spire demolished in 1706. After some 90 yards turn right onto path SP19, a rough lane bounded by stone walls and follow it bearing left to a gate and stile into a field. Cross the stile and go straight on down the field. By the far corner of the churchyard wall turn right onto path SP17 to cross a stile by an ivy-clad tree. Now turn left onto bridleway SP16 crossing a cattle grid then turn right through gates into a field crossing a corner to a bend in the right-hand hedge. Here follow the hedge downhill to a bridlegate and bridge in the bottom corner then keep straight on to pass through a second bridlegate. Now turn right and follow a right-hand hedge to a corner of the field then turn left and follow a right-hand fence, later a hedge, uphill, ignoring a stile in the fence, to reach a bridlegate into Grove Lane, Dean.

Turn left onto this road which becomes unsurfaced. After 200 yards turn right through a bridlegate by a field gate (still on SP16). Now keep left of a fence bearing slightly left across a field gradually diverging from the fence and passing just left of an electricity pole, with a fine view to your right towards Chadlington, to reach a gap in the bottom hedge. Do NOT go through this but turn sharp left onto the Oxfordshire Way (path SP20) across the field to cross a stile by a bridlegate in the left-hand hedge. Now turn left and follow the left-hand hedge with fine views of the Evenlode valley to your right, wiggling to your right at one point to reach a stone track at the far side of the field. Turn right onto this and follow it descending gently for a third of a mile past Dean Grove to your left then look out for a left-hand stile. Cross this and bear half left across a field to cross a stile and footbridge by some willows left of a bend in a stream. Now take path CB2 bearing slightly right across a field to a corner of a fence then follow the left-hand fence straight on to cross a stile by a gate. Follow the edge of the spinney straight on then continue across a field corner to cross a stile. Now follow a left-hand hedge straight on through two fields to a stile into a green lane called Watery Lane (CB1). Turn right into this lane then at a left-hand bend bear slightly right over a stile onto a permissive path to a bridge over the mill stream of the River Evenlode. (N.B. If the permissive path is closed, an alternative route via definitive rights of way is shown on the map.) Cross this bridge and turn left onto a worn path along the island with fine views towards Charlbury ahead. On reaching Charlbury Mill, go through a kissing-gate and cross a bridge then follow a rough lane uphill to the B4437 onto which you turn right for the station.

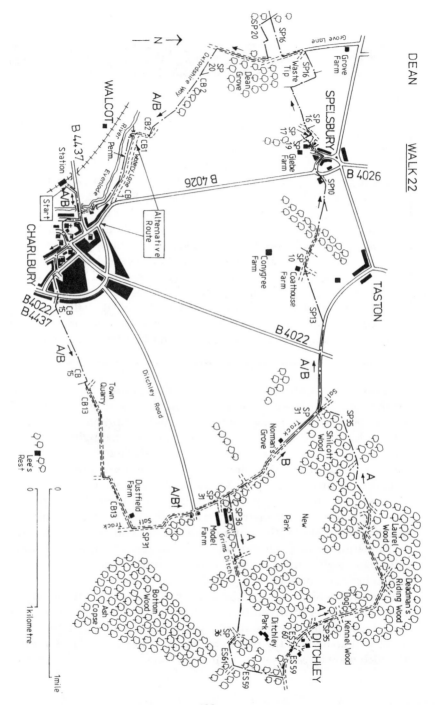

WALK 23 :   STONESFIELD

Length of Walk: 7.2 miles / 11.6 Km
Starting Point: Entrance to Stonesfield Village Hall.
Grid Ref: SP395175
Maps: OS Landranger Sheet 164
OS Pathfinder Sheet 1091 (SP21/31)

How to get there / Parking: Stonesfield, 3 miles west of Woodstock, may be reached from the town by taking the A44 towards Chipping Norton and Evesham. After 2 miles by the 'Duke of Marlborough' turn left onto the B4437 towards Charlbury. At a sharp right-hand bend, fork left onto a road signposted to Combe and Stonesfield and keep straight on to Stonesfield. On entering the village, take the first turning right (Greenfield Road) and follow it (later as Longore) until the village hall is signposted to your right. Here either turn right for the village hall car park or use a parking bay on the left a few yards further on.

Notes: Flooding is possible near the Evenlode after heavy rain.

Stonesfield, on a hilltop above the Evenlode valley, is best known for the slate which was quarried and mined there up to 1909 and was popular for roofing due to its light, non-porous nature. Although most of the quarrying took place in the eighteenth and nineteenth centuries, it is believed to have started in Roman times and indeed Roman settlement of the area has been proved by the discovery of the sites of three Roman villas around the parish. Two of these had decorated pavements but after their discovery the pavements were unfortunately destroyed by ploughing. The village, which is also close to a Roman road called Akeman Street, today has a thirteenth-century church and a number of attractive stone cottages ranged along a maze of narrow winding lanes but has been somewhat marred by modern 'infill' development.

The walk, which explores the hills on either side of this beautiful narrow section of the Evenlode valley, is one of fine views and great variety including woodland, old green lanes and quiet riverside scenery. It also visits the quiet hamlets of Wilcote and Fawler, both of which were already settled in Roman times.

Starting from the entrance to Stonesfield Village Hall, turn right into Longore and follow it to a T-junction. Here turn left into a winding village street called Pond Hill. After 350 yards, where the priority road turns sharp left, fork right into Church Street passing the 'Black Head'. At a small square at the junction with High Street, turn right onto path ST7 heading towards the church. Go past the former village lock-up into the churchyard. Now pass left of the church and continue through the churchyard to a stone stile leading to a road called Church Fields. Turn left onto this road then just past a house called 'Stocky View', turn immediately right into a green lane to the old slate quarries (path ST5) and follow it downhill out of the village. By a small green building called 'Andy's Den' fork right down some steps in an old quarry face to cross a stile then go straight on down a field to a stile into the corner of Stockey Plantation. In this wood bear slightly left up a bank to join path FW6 then take it straight on along the inside edge of the wood. At the far end of the wood turn left onto path NL37, a green lane on the line of Akeman Street, the Roman road from London via Bicester to Cirencester. After 60 yards turn right onto bridleway ST4 following a left-hand fence downhill to cross a footbridge over the River Evenlode by Stonesfield Ford.

Now take bridleway NL1 straight on across a field to gates in the next hedge. Go through these then turn right through a hedge gap and follow worn path NL2 close to the banks of the Evenlode for three-quarters of a mile, after a quarter mile passing under a railway bridge then continuing through Whitehall Wood until you reach a squeeze-stile which leads in 40 yards to a road. Turn right onto this road then at a crossroads turn left onto the North Leigh and Witney road. After 100 yards fork left onto bridleway NL33, a pleasant green lane beside a stream along a valley bottom lined with daffodils in Spring and follow it for a third of a mile. At a left-hand bend where Holly Court Farm comes into view ahead, turn sharp right through a hedge gap onto path NL5 heading for the near corner of a hedge on the hillside. Now follow this left-hand hedge straight on over a rise, later with views over your right shoulder back towards Stonesfield, to reach gates onto a road.

Turn left onto this road then fork immediately right onto a side road. After some 70 yards turn left through a hedge gap onto the continuation of path NL5 and head for the farmhouse at Bridewell Farm to reach a gap in the bottom hedge. Here cross a stream and aim for the left-hand end of the farm buildings to reach a track junction at the entrance to the farmyard. Now bear slightly left to a hedge gap on the bank of a stream. Go through this then turn right (still on path NL5) following a right-hand hedge uphill. Where the hedge ends, bear slightly left across the field to a gap in the next hedge then bear half right downhill to cross a stile by the corner of another hedge. Now follow a raised fenced track across a marshy area called Lady Well to some gates. Here take a grassy track straight on uphill along an avenue of ancient pollarded ash trees with fine views opening out to your right towards Stonesfield, over your right shoulder towards Church Hanborough church spire, Wytham Hill and the distant Chilterns beyond and behind you towards North Leigh Church with its Saxon tower. Now continue through a copse and on approaching Wilcote Grange, turn left through gates onto a fenced track. Follow this track through a series of gates, briefly with a concrete surface, later ignoring a grassy track merging from the left and passing through a gate onto a macadam road at Wilcote, onto which you turn left.

At a T-junction turn right onto a road through Wilcote past its mainly fourteenth-century church with an earlier chancel arch and Norman doorway and Wilcote Grange to your right. At a left-hand bend by the gates to the manor house, turn left over a stile onto path NL5 beside a left-hand hedge, crossing the barely perceptible line of Akeman Street then following the edge of Sumteth's Copse downhill. About halfway down the wood bear half right across the field to a stile in its bottom right-hand corner onto a road called Wilcote Riding. Turn left onto this road then at a left-hand bend turn right through the gates to Hunts Copse onto bridleway FS9 taking a track straight on past farm buildings to enter Topples Wood. In the wood take the track straight on, ignoring branching tracks to your left then your right and gradually bearing left. On entering a field with fine views towards Fawler to your right, fork left onto a track following the edge of the wood at first then continuing as a narrow green lane downhill into the valley bottom. Here at a left-hand bend turn right over two stiles onto path FS8 along the valley bottom to the banks of the Evenlode then turn right over a stile and follow the riverbank. On nearing a railway bridge, turn left over a new footbridge specially built by Oxfordshire County Council for this walk then turn right onto path FW5 passing under the railway bridge and continuing

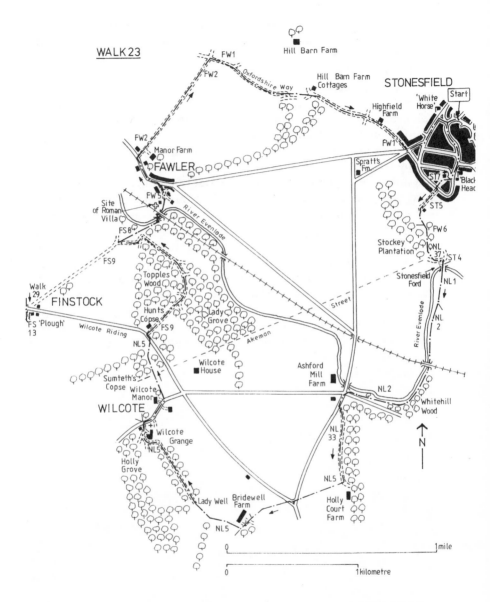

across a field to a gate and stile under a powerline. Now take a rough lane straight on uphill through the hamlet of Fawler, a settlement created in a clearing in Wychwood Forest in the twelfth century.

At a T-junction turn left onto a road. After 300 yards, just past a farm to your left, turn right onto bridleway FW2, a concrete road. Where its surface ends, take a stone-based green lane straight on uphill for a quarter mile with views towards Finstock opening out behind. On entering a field, take a grassy track straight on beside a left-hand stone wall. At the far end of the field go through a hedge gap then turn right onto bridleway FW1, joining the Oxfordshire Way and following a grassy track beside a right-hand hedge. After over a third of a mile where the track turns right through the hedge, leave it and go straight on through a bridlegate. Now follow the right-hand hedge uphill to gates near Hill Barn Farm Cottages, then keep straight on uphill joining a farm road. At the top of the hill Stonesfield comes into view ahead and wide views open out to your right towards Wytham Hill and North Leigh. At a crossways take bridleway FW1 straight on, descending into Stonesfield. On reaching a road, turn left onto it, climbing Laughton Hill and continuing along The Ridings then, just before the 'White Horse', fork right and at a staggered crossroads take Longore straight on to reach your starting point.

WALK 24: KIDDINGTON

Length of Walk:	6.5 miles / 10.5 Km
Starting Point:	Over Kiddington crossroads.
Grid Ref:	SP410221
Maps:	OS Landranger Sheet 164
	OS Pathfinder Sheets 1069 (SP42/52)
	& 1092 (SP 41/51)

How to get there / Parking: Over Kiddington, 4 miles northwest of Woodstock, may be reached from the town by taking the A44 towards Chipping Norton and Evesham. Just before reaching the crossroads at Over Kiddington, park in a layby on the right.

Kiddington, known to most people as merely a cluster of cottages straddling an A44 crossroads, in fact consists of two distinct hamlets on either side of the Glyme valley separated by Kiddington Park. Over Kiddington, on the ridgetop followed by the A44 in typical Cotswold fashion, has an interesting old stone cross and is half a mile east of the site of the lost mediaeval village of Asterleigh. This village, whose name indicates that it was created by forest clearance, comprised twenty farms in 1279 but was abandoned in the fifteenth century probably due to the impoverishment of the soil and is now no more than a large farm. Although Asterleigh lost separate parochial status in 1466, this is still reflected in the parish name of Kiddington with Asterleigh. Nether Kiddington, in a northern combe of the beautiful Glyme valley, is a quiet sleepy place with picturesque Cotswold-stone cottages in leafy surroundings on the edge of the park containing the imposing Kiddington Hall and the twelfth-century parish church, much altered in the fourteenth century when its tower was constructed.

The walk, which is of an easy nature, explores this well-wooded part of the Oxfordshire Cotswolds passing the sites of two Roman villas before crossing the A44 and following the beautiful Glyme valley with some fine views through both Glympton Park and Kiddington Park and returning to Over Kiddington.

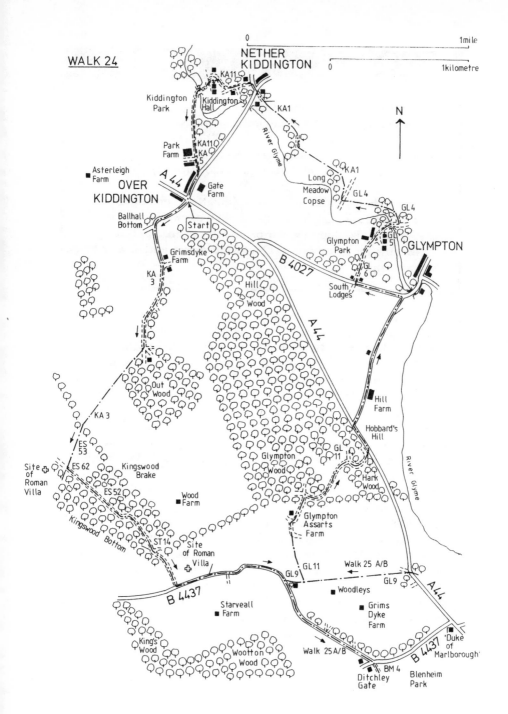

WALK 24

Starting from the crossroads in Over Kiddington, take the Ditchley road downhill into Ballhall Bottom. Here turn left onto the road to Grimsdyke Farm. At the farm take the road (now bridleway KA3) straight on for a further third of a mile until it enters Out Wood. Here turn right onto a crossing track passing through a gate and following the outside edge of the wood then a left-hand fence straight on to a bridlegate in a thick hedge. Go through this then bear half left onto bridleway ES53 heading for where a mixed plantation gives way to a coniferous one at the edge of a wood called Kingswood Brake near the site of a fourth-century Roman villa with a large granary. Here turn left onto bridleway ES62, a grassy track along the outside edge of the wood which soon enters it and becomes ES52, looking out for signs giving the dates at which the various plantations were planted. Take the track straight on through the woods for half a mile, eventually dropping into Kingswood Bottom and crossing a stone bridge, then (as bridleway ST14) joining a macadam farm road at a hairpin bend and taking it straight on uphill out of the wood to reach the B4437.

Turn left onto this road and follow it for half a mile passing the site of another Roman villa in a field to your left. On rounding a blind right-hand bend, fork immediately left onto path GL9 between a hedge and a copse, joining the reverse direction of **Walk 25** and soon emerging into a field by the back of Woodleys Cottages. Here go straight on along the edge of the field to a gate. Do NOT go through this, but turn left onto path GL11 leaving **Walk 25** again and following a right-hand hedge. At the far end of the hedge join a concrete farm road and keep straight on towards Glympton Assarts Farm ('assarts' being an old word for a cultivated place in a forest). Where the road forks, bear right continuing to follow it downhill past the farm to gates into Glympton Wood. At a three-way fork just inside the wood turn right onto a track climbing steeply through woodland to reach a gate. Now take the track straight on over a hill beside a right-hand hedge to a track junction by a gate in the valley bottom. Here fork right passing through the gate and soon swinging left uphill to a gate and rails leading to the A44.

Turn left onto its walkable nearside verge and follow it to Glympton Turn. Here turn right and take the Glympton road for over half a mile past Hill Farm then with views of the Glyme valley to your right. On reaching a T-junction just outside Glympton, a picturesque

Cotswold-stone estate village to your right, turn left onto the B4027 and follow it uphill beside Glympton Park wall for a quarter mile to reach South Lodges. Turn right through the ornamental gates onto path GL6 and take this fenced drive descending gradually to a bridge over a ha-ha, with views to your right of a lake created by damming the River Glyme. Where the drive forks, keep left passing left of the house, briefly home of the Australian tycoon Alan Bond, and the rebuilt Norman Church and now on path GL5, bearing right to cross a bridge over the River Glyme.

About 60 yards beyond this bridge turn left onto path GL4, a grassy track and follow it uphill into a copse. Where the track ends, ignore a stile in iron railings ahead and bear half left taking a winding path through the trees to two white gates. Go through both gates then keep straight on across a parkland field to join a left-hand fence at its second kink and follow it crossing a track to reach a belt of trees at the far side of the field. Here enter a tree belt then turn right following a path through it until you emerge into another field. Now turn left along the edge of the tree belt soon passing through an area of scrub. (If the path through the scrub is impassable, follow the edge of the field round it.) On re-emerging into the field, follow a left-hand hedge straight on. Where this hedge turns away to the left, leave it and go straight on across the field to a hedge gap leading into a green lane. At the far end of this lane bear slightly left along the outside edge of a belt of scrub. Where the scrub ends, keep straight on across the field, heading just right of the left-hand of two electricity poles ahead to reach the end of a grassy track which leads you downhill through some trees to join a macadam drive and reach a road junction in Nether Kiddington.

Here cross the priority road and go straight on. At a fork bear slightly left onto the drive to Kiddington Hall (path KA11) passing between ornamental gateposts. Ignore a branching drive to the left, then at a fork about 120 yards short of the Hall, take the right-hand option signposted to the church. Follow this drive straight on past the church. Just before reaching the gate to a cottage, turn left through a hedge gap onto a grassy track ignoring a crossing path then bearing half left past the church and a dovecote to your left and gradually bearing right to cross a bridge over a lake formed in the River Glyme. Now bear half left onto a grassy track beside a right-hand fence, with fine views of Kiddington Hall to your left, to a gate into a copse. Take the track straight on uphill through the copse and along an avenue of trees to a gate by a cottage. Now take a macadam drive straight on, joining bridleway KA5, to reach gates onto Over Kiddington village street by the old cross, then turn right onto it for your starting point.

WALK 25 :   WOODSTOCK

Length of Walk: (A) 8.8 miles / 14.2 Km
                      (B) 6.7 miles / 10.7 Km
                      (C) 4.7 miles / 7.5 Km
Starting Point: Crossroads by 'Punchbowl Inn', Woodstock.
Grid Ref: SP446167
Maps: OS Landranger Sheet 164
                      OS Pathfinder Sheet 1092 (SP41/51)
Parking: Free car park in Hensington Road signposted from the A44.
Notes: All the paths used in Blenheim Park are public rights of
     way, so no admission charges are payable if you keep to the
     described walk routes.

Woodstock (or New Woodstock as it has traditionally been known)
just outside the wall of Blenheim Park was established as a new
market town by Henry II in about 1163 to provide services for his
men during his stays at his hunting lodge in Woodstock Park (as
Blenheim was then known) and for much of the Middle Ages was
only second in importance within the county to Oxford. Its church
was originally built at about the same time, but has been
substantially altered over the centuries notably by the rebuilding of
its tower in 1785. Woodstock Park remained in royal hands until
1704 and witnessed the legendary courtship of Henry II and Fair
Rosamond, the birth of the Black Prince and the imprisonment of
the future Elizabeth I by Mary Tudor in 1554. In 1704, however, it
was presented by Queen Anne to John Churchill, 1st Duke of
Marlborough, in recognition of his victories in the War of Spanish
Succession notably at the Battle of Blenheim in Bavaria, after which
the park was renamed. There then followed the construction at
public expense of Blenheim Palace designed by Sir John Vanbrugh
and the demolition of the former royal palace which had been badly
damaged during the Civil War and in the 1760s Capability Brown
undertook the landscaping of the Park including the damming of
the River Glyme to form the lake which has since formed the
spectacular focal point of this masterpiece of eighteenth-century
landscape architecture.

All three walks commence in Woodstock and take in parts of Blenheim Park while Walks A and B additionally explore the rolling hills to the north surrounding the Glyme valley and skirt the picturesque stone-built village of Wootton dominated by its fine thirteenth-century church.

Walks A and B start by the 'Punchbowl Inn' at the junction of Oxford Street (A44), Hensington Road and Market Place and take the A44 northwestwards towards Evesham. At a left-hand bend turn right into Upper Brook Hill following it for a quarter mile ignoring all side turnings. Where the priority road turns sharp right, leave it and take bridleway HW3, a macadam road straight on towards Woodstock Lawn Cemetery with the buildings to your left soon giving way to marshland flanking the River Glyme. After over a third of a mile, where the macadam road turns right into Woodstock Sewage Works, leave it and take an old green lane narrowed by encroaching scrub straight on for half a mile, eventually joining bridleway HW2 and entering a field. Here fork left through a bridlegate and follow a sporadic left-hand hedge to a bridlegate onto the B4027, the ancient London–Worcester road near Sansom's Farm. Turn left onto this road then, at its junction with Akeman Street, a Roman Road from London via Bicester to Cirencester, and the Oxfordshire Way just past some cottages, bear half left over a stile onto path WO2a and cross a field diagonally heading just left of the slate roof of Hordley Farm to reach a small gate. Go through this then bear slightly right to a gate under lime trees right of the old farmhouse.

Hordley, today little more than a farm, marks the site of a lost village which in 1279 counted 19 households and had its own chapel, but appears by the sixteenth-century to have shrunk to its present size. The present Hordley Farm, built by John Gregory in about 1600, has a quadrangular layout typical of mediaeval times suggesting that it may be built on older foundations.

Turn left onto the farm drive (bridleway WO2). In the former farmyard bear slightly right onto a path through the trees passing right of a pool in the River Glyme to cross a bridge over the river. Now go through a gate and across a meadow to a bridlegate between ash trees then follow a left-hand hedge straight on, with Wootton briefly coming into view to your right before you enter an old overgrown green lane. At the far end of this lane go through a bridlegate with Wootton coming into view ahead and go straight on past a cottage. Near the far side of the field turn left onto path WO4 crossing a stile by a gate. On reaching the cottage drive (path WO17), turn right onto it and take it straight on for a quarter mile to a road at West End on the edge of Wootton.

Turn left onto the road then immediately right up a steep bank onto path WO1 turning right and following a right-hand stone wall, later a fence to a corner of the field. Now turn left still beside a right-hand fence with fine views to your right of Wootton and later an artificial lake in the Glyme valley. At the far end of the field turn left then immediately right through a hedge gap. Now follow a right-hand hedge straight on (later on path GL10). At the far end of the field turn left ignoring wooden rails into a plantation. After about 25 yards turn right over a stile and take a winding path through the plantation to a stile leading to a blind bend on the A44. Cross this road carefully, keeping left of a chevron sign immediately opposite then go straight on through a hedge gap onto fenced path GL9. On entering a right-hand field, follow its left-hand hedge straight on to a corner. Here go straight on through a belt of trees concealing Grim's Ditch then take a fenced path straight on past a landfill site to a stile into a field. Now follow the left-hand hedge straight on, passing through a New Zealand (barbed-wire) gate and later a five-bar gate where you join the reverse direction of **Walk 24**. Here continue past a row of cottages then bear slightly left into a path between hedges passing a small copse in an old stonepit to reach the B4437.

Turn left onto this road, leaving **Walk 24** again. Follow the road for over half a mile to a junction at Ditchley Gate. Here leave the road and take path BM4 straight on through the gates into Blenheim Park with the Column of Victory and Blenheim Palace coming into view at the far end of a wide recently replanted avenue of trees. (N.B. The gates have two concealed latches which have to be operated simultaneously to open them.) Now follow the macadam drive straight on along this avenue for over three-quarters of a mile ignoring the branching drive to North Lodge and Akeman Street and the Oxfordshire Way which cross it at the first cattle grid. Some 200 yards beyond the second cattle grid at a slight dip in the drive, **Walk A** turns right off it to pass through a gap in the fence. Now omit the next two paragraphs.

Walk B continues along the macadam drive soon on path BM2, eventually bearing left out of the avenue and entering a valley with some enormous ancient beeches and other fine parkland trees. On nearing a cottage, keep left at two forks. Now read the last paragraph.

Walk C also starts by the 'Punchbowl Inn' at the junction of Oxford Street (A44), Hensington Road and Market Place and takes the A44 northwestwards towards Evesham for a third of a mile, descending a hill to cross a bridge over the River Glyme. Now fork left onto bridleway WS2 through the green gates of No.95, turning left again through the smaller of two gates to enter Blenheim Park. Here turn right onto a macadam drive (bridleway BM2) and follow it for nearly a mile, at first along a valley with fine ancient beeches then bearing left to reach a wide tree-lined avenue into which it turns right. In a slight dip some 200 yards short of a crossing fenceline with a cattle grid turn left onto path BM4 through a fence gap.

Walks A and C now take path BM4 bearing slightly right to join a left-hand fence and follow it to a gate in it. Turn left through this and take an ill-defined grassy track straight on across the field passing right of a chestnut copse. By this copse leave the track and bear half right to a rail-stile in a right-hand fence. Do NOT cross this, but bear half left and follow the fence circling a copper beech copse and continuing to a stile onto a macadam drive by an entrance to Park Farm. Turn left onto this drive bearing right then turning left and soon passing between woods. Where the drive forks, turn right (still on path BM4) descending past some ancient beeches then bearing left, crossing a cattle grid and bearing right. At the far end of this right-hand bend turn sharp left onto path BM5, an ill-defined grassy track and follow it to cross a stile near the end of an arm of the lake. Now go straight on passing left of some tall trees. At a three-way fork bear right onto path BM7, a stony track along the shore of the lake. After a third of a mile, on rounding a left-hand bend, fine views open out across the lake towards Grand Bridge, also the work of Vanbrugh, backed by Woodstock Church and Blenheim Palace partially hidden by trees. Now ignore a branching track to your right and go past Fair Rosamond's Well, a spring surrounded by iron railings below you.

On reaching a macadam drive (path BM6), Grand Bridge (the end of the public footpath) is to your right where there is a good view of the façade of the Palace. Otherwise turn left onto this drive and follow it for a third of a mile. At the far end of a left-hand enclosure in a slight dip turn right onto path BM5 following a left-hand fence towards the Column of Victory. Where the fence turns left, leave it and go straight on past the Column then between fenced enclosures to pass just left of a cottage in a dip crossing two macadam drives and turning right onto a third (bridleway BM2).

Walks A, B and C now take this drive for 350 yards, soon with Queen Pool to your right, until you reach some green gates to your left. Turn left through the smaller of these onto bridleway WS2 turning right through more gates onto the A44 at Old Woodstock. Turn right onto this road crossing the River Glyme. Just past a cottage called 'The Old Bakery' turn right onto Hoggrove Hill, a path up a flight of steps. On reaching a bend in a road, take Chaucer's Lane straight on uphill then at a T-junction turn left into Park Street and follow it past the church and County Museum. Where the road forks, keep right passing right of the eighteenth-century Town Hall and continuing to your starting point.

WALK 25

'Killingworth Castle'
B4027
WOOTTON
Hark Wood
Glympton Assarts Farm
Worcester Hill
River Glyme
Home Farm
River Dorn
A44
Grim's Ditch
A/B
Walk 24
GL11
GL9
GL 10
WO1
WO1
WO17
WO 4
IWO
WO 2
WO 2
HORDLEY
B4027
Woodleys
Grim's Dyke Farm
B4437
B4437
'Duke of Marlborough'
Akeman Street
WO 2a
Sansom's Farm HW2
Ditchley Gate
BM4
Akeman Street
River Glyme
HW 2
HW 3
North Lodge
Furze Platt
Blenheim
A/B
N
BM 4
BM2
A/C
C
B
Park Farm
OLD WOODSTOCK
Sewage Works
A/B
HW 3
'Rose & Crown'
'Black Prince'
Column of Victory
Park
BM5
WOODSTOCK
BM2
Queen Pool
WS 2
CP
'Punchbowl Inn'
BM5
A/C
A/B/C
Start
A44
BM4
BM5
BM6
BM 7
BM7
Grand Bridge
Fair Rosamonds Well
The Lake
Blenheim Palace

0   1 mile

0   1 kilometre

149

WALK 26 :   YARNTON / BLADON

Length of Walk: (A)   8.0 miles / 12.9 Km
                               (B)   3.3 miles / 5.3 Km
                               (C)   4.7 miles / 7.6 Km
Starting Point: (A/B)   Yarnton Church.
                               (C)   Entrance to 'Lamb' car park, Bladon.
Grid Ref: (A/B) SP478117 / (C) SP448146
Maps: OS Landranger Sheet 164
                            OS Pathfinder Sheet 1092 (SP41/51)

How to get there / Parking: (A/B) Yarnton, 4 miles northwest
of Oxford, may be reached from the Peartree Roundabout on
the Oxford Ring Road by taking the A44 towards Woodstock
and Evesham for 1 mile. At the second roundabout turn left
onto a road signposted to Cassington. After half a mile turn
left into Church Lane and follow it for some 400 yards to a
parking area on the left opposite the church. In the interests
of other users, be sure to park at right angles to the road!
(C) Bladon, 7 miles northwest of Oxford, may be reached
from the Peartree Roundabout by taking the A44 towards
Woodstock and Evesham for 3.7 miles. At the Bladon
Roundabout turn left onto the A4095 towards Witney.
Follow it through Bladon for 1 mile, then 180 yards beyond
the 'Lamb', turn left into Manor Road and follow it round a
left-hand bend to a signposted car park at a right-hand bend.
N.B. This is the 'Lamb' car park but non-customers may use
it.

Yarnton is thought of today by many as a suburban satellite of
Oxford to be passed in haste on the A44, yet the original village
with its church and manor house down its cul-de-sac lane south of
Cassington Road remains a quiet rural idyll and seems like another
world. The Jacobean manor house was built in 1612 by Sir Thomas
Spencer, an ancestor of Diana, Princess of Wales, whose family lived
there for 100 years until it was sold in 1712. The nearby Norman
church, which had been much altered and enlarged in the thirteenth
century, was also restored at the same time by Sir Thomas Spencer

who had its tower rebuilt and the Spencer Chapel added, in which there are two magnificent baroque family tombs.

Bladon, an attractive Cotswold-stone village just outside the wall of Blenheim Park, came to national prominence in 1965 when Sir Winston Churchill's body was brought by special train to nearby Hanborough Station for burial with other family members in the churchyard. At one time mother church for Woodstock, Bladon Church was demolished and rebuilt at the Duke of Marlborough's expense in 1804 and subsequently heavily restored by Sir Reginald Blomfield in 1891 and is now a regular tourist attraction.

All three walks lead you to Spring Hill, a low rise northwest of Yarnton with wide views across the Thames valley with Walks A and B visiting the hamlet of Worton and the former Yarnton railway junction while Walks A and C explore the Bladon and Begbroke areas.

Walks A and B start in Church Lane, Yarnton near the church and manor house and follow it back to its junction with Cassington Road. Cross this road, turn left along its far pavement and follow it straight on past the 'Red Lion' for a quarter mile. After the pavement ends and you pass the speed delimiting sign, at a left-hand bend fork right onto path Y14, a stony lane. Having passed a bungalow to your left, go straight on into an old green lane called Frogwelldown Lane and continue along it for over half a mile until you emerge over a footbridge into a field. Here follow a right-hand hedge straight on uphill, soon with views towards Wytham Hill and Cassington Church opening out to your left. After crossing the top of Spring Hill, at a gap in the right-hand hedge where you can see a newly-restored cottage to your right, **Walk B** turns left onto path Y15. Now omit the next four paragraphs.

Walks A and C now take path Y14 straight on beside the right-hand hedge through two fields with a fine view towards Church Hanborough with its prominent church spire ahead. At the far side of the second field go straight on through a hedge gap then bear half right onto path CA7 still following a right-hand hedge. By the ruins of a stone barn bear half left across the field heading for an oak tree and Church Hanborough spire to cross a footbridge and stile just right of the oak tree then follow a left-hand hedge. At the far end of the field *ignore a gateway ahead* and turn right then immediately left over a stile.

Now follow a left-hand hedge to cross a stile at the far end of the field. Bear slightly left across the next field to a corner of a wood ahead called Bladon Heath. Here bear slightly right onto path BD8 along the outside edge of the wood eventually turning left to a gate and stile onto a road. Turn right onto this road passing Burleigh Lodge, rounding a left-hand bend and continuing beside Burleigh Wood with a view towards woods in Blenheim Park ahead. At a right-hand bend turn right over a stile onto path BD6 following a left-hand hedge to cross a footbridge and rails. Now turn left and follow a left-hand hedge, later a ditch to a corner of the field. Here turn right keeping right of a hedge and passing through an old gateway, then follow a left-hand hedge gently uphill to gates and a stile onto a bend in Manor Road, Bladon. Take this road straight on to the entrance of the 'Lamb' car park at a right-hand bend (the starting point of Walk C).

Walks A and C now take the continuation of Manor Road to its junction with Heath Lane. Here cross Heath Lane and bear half left into Church Street, keeping right at a fork to reach a lychgate into the churchyard. Go straight on through this gate and take a concrete path passing left of the church and the graves of Sir Winston Churchill and a number of his relatives and continuing to wrought-iron gates at the far end of the churchyard. Now turn right onto macadam path BD2. Where its surface ends, follow its gravel then grassy continuation straight on to a crossways at the far end of the left-hand field. Here turn right onto path BD3 following a left-hand hedge. By a copse called Withy Clump you enter a green lane and continue to an old iron gate by some garages.

Here turn left onto path BD4, normally a crop-break, and follow it generally parallel to the right-hand hedge to a hedge gap right of an oak tree at the far end of the field. Now keep straight on, heading just left of the distant Beckley radio and TV mast to a hedge gap at the far end of the field then bear slightly right across the next field to a hedge gap at the left-hand end of a sporadic line of trees. Here take path BG5 straight on heading for a gap between tall trees right of Begbroke Church to cross a stile. Now pass left of a tall oak tree to reach a stile into an enclosed path leading to a gravel drive. Turn left onto this drive and follow it to the end of a road by Begbroke Church, a Norman building with a tower with a saddleback roof.

Take this road to a T-junction opposite a large stone office building, formerly a convent. Here turn right into Spring Hill Road and follow

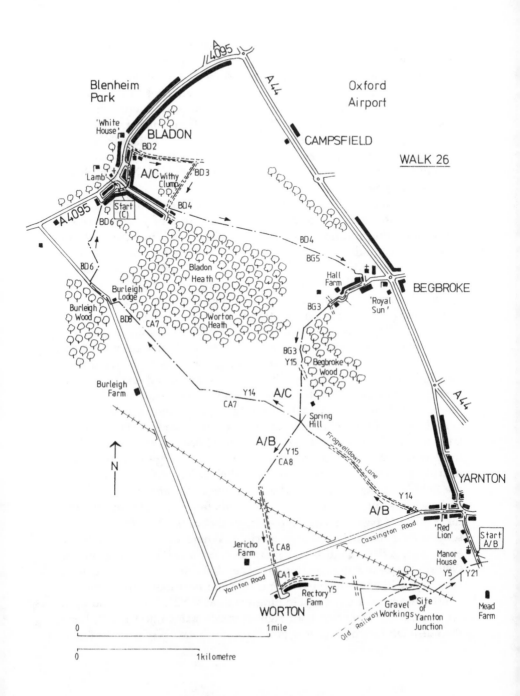

Blenheim Park

'White House'

BLADON

BD2

'Lamb'

A/C Withy Clump

BD3

Start (C)

BD4

BD6

A4095

BD6

Burleigh Lodge

Bladon Heath

Burleigh Wood

BD8

CA7

Worton Heath

Burleigh Farm

N

Y14

CA7

A/C

Spring Hill

A/B

Y15

CA8

Jericho Farm

CA8

Worton Road

CA1

WORTON

Rectory Farm

Y5

A4095

A44

Oxford Airport

CAMPSFIELD

WALK 26

BD4

BG5

Hall Farm

BEGBROKE

BG3

'Royal Sun'

BG3

Y15

Begbroke Wood

Frogwelldown Lane

Y14

A/B

A44

YARNTON

Cassington Road

'Red Lion'

Start A/B

Manor House

Y5

Y21

Gravel Workings

Site of Yarnton Junction

Old Railway

Mead Farm

0 _____ 1 mile

0 _____ 1 kilometre

153

its winding course to its end then take path BG3 straight on over a stile by gates and a cattle grid. Now, leaving the farm road, head for the far end of Begbroke Wood to your left then bear half left across the field to another corner of the wood where Wytham Hill comes into view ahead. Here follow the edge of the wood (soon on path Y15) to cross a stile by gates and a cattle grid on a farm road. Leaving the farm road, go straight on across two fields towards Wytham Hill to go through a hedge gap right of an electricity pole on the next rise (Spring Hill). Here **Walk C** turns right onto path Y14. Now go back four paragraphs.

Walks A and B take path Y15 straight across the field aiming right of Cassington Church to a hedge gap by a clump of willow bushes. Go through this and take path CA8 straight on, still heading right of Cassington Church to a hedge gap in the far corner of the field. Here join a concrete road and follow it for nearly half a mile passing Cassington Sewage Works and crossing a bridge over the Oxford–Worcester railway line. On reaching a road junction, cross the major road and take a side road straight on towards Worton.

By the village postbox turn left onto path CA1 along a concrete road past the ornamental gates to Rectory Farm. In the farmyard take a farm road straight on between buildings and past a manege then bear half right over a stile by a blue gate into a fenced enclosure and cross a series of stiles to pass through a tree-belt and cross a footbridge. Now take path Y5 bearing slightly right across a large field, heading for a green barn to reach a rough road by the corner of an earth bund screening gravel workings. Cross this road and follow the left side of the bund straight on along the edge of a field. On nearing a copse of poplars ahead, bear slightly left across the corner of the field, entering the left-hand edge of the copse and soon joining a plain-wire railway fence. Now follow this fence straight on through the copse and past the barn on the site of the former Yarnton Junction, soon with a second fence to your right. Where the right-hand fence ends, turn left through a fence gap to cross a level-crossing on the Oxford–Worcester line. At the far side of the track turn right, then after about 20 yards turn left over a stile and bear half right following a left-hand line of trees. On joining bridleway Y21, follow it straight on, soon with a fence to your right to reach gates into Church Lane then turn left for your starting point.

Length of Walk:	(A) 7.5 miles / 12.1 Km
	(B) 4.1 miles / 6.5 Km
Starting Point:	'Cock Inn', Combe village green.
Grid Ref:	SP412159
Maps:	OS Landranger Sheet 164
	OS Pathfinder Sheet 1092 (SP41/51)

How to get there / Parking: Combe, 2 miles southwest of
   Woodstock, may be reached from the town by taking the A44
   towards Chipping Norton and Evesham. After 2 miles by the
   'Duke of Marlborough' turn left onto the B4437 towards
   Charlbury. At a sharp right-hand bend, fork left onto a road
   signposted to Combe and Stonesfield. After 1 mile turn left
   onto a road signposted to Combe and Hanborough and
   follow it for 1.4 miles to Combe village green. Here fork left
   and park beside the stone wall on the north side of the green.

Combe, with its Cotswold-stone cottages ranged around a spacious
village green on a hilltop plateau, differs markedly from what its
name might lead one to expect as 'combe' or 'coomb' usually means
a short valley cutting into a hillside. The reason for this is that, like
some other mediaeval villages, Combe was moved uphill from the
Evenlode valley in the mid-fourteenth century probably to provide
easier access from the village to new arable fields which had been
cleared on the plateau. Evidence of this is provided by the church
which was moved to the new village in 1395 as, unlike many village
churches which were first built in stone in the Norman period and
subsequently 'modernised' in later centuries, Combe Church was
newly built in the Perpendicular style of the period and has
remained largely unaltered till the present day, thus giving it an
unusually uniform appearance.

   Both walks lead you from Combe to explore the beautiful narrow
winding section of the Evenlode valley to the south of the village
where the original village must have been, while Walk A
additionally circles, but largely avoids the straggling suburban
villages of Long Hanborough and Freeland to visit the beautiful

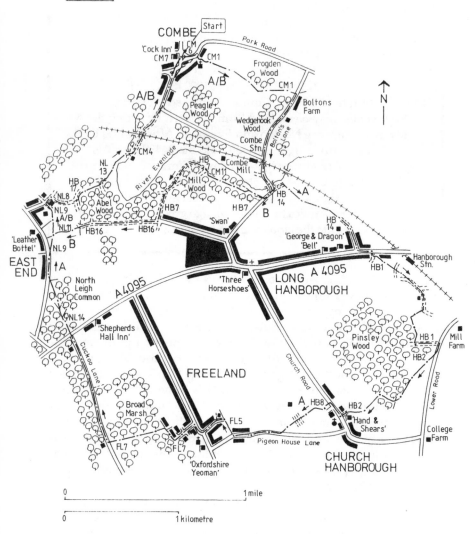

rural village of Church Hanborough and explore the pleasant surrounding hills with their generous scattering of woodland.

Both walks start from the 'Cock Inn' at Combe village green and take path CM6 straight across the green to a road junction by an oak tree in the far corner. Here take Park Road straight on, soon forking right by a telephone box under a fine cedar tree onto path CM1 leading to Combe Church. Go through gates into the churchyard then turn left onto a stony path passing left of the church to reach a squeeze stile formed by old gravestones leading onto the recreation ground. Here follow a right-hand hedge straight on then bear slightly right through an area of trees to a hedge gap into a field. Now bear half left across the field, with a brief view towards the Hanboroughs to your right, to reach a hedge gap in the bottom of a dip then bear slightly right across the next field to join and follow the right-hand edge of Frogden Wood. At a corner of the field go straight on through a hedge gap then turn left, still following the edge of Frogden Wood, later a hedge to a corner of the field. Here go through a hedge gap and bear slightly left across a field heading for the corner of a garden hedge left of Boltons Farm to cross a rail stile into Bolton's Lane. Turn right onto this road and follow it downhill for some 700 yards with Long Hanborough coming into view ahead. At the bottom of the hill near Combe Station on the Oxford–Worcester railway, ignore a branching road to the right, pass under a railway bridge and cross a bridge over the River Evenlode. At a sharp right-hand bend **Walk A** turns left onto bridleway HB14. Now omit the next two paragraphs.

Walk B continues to follow the road round the bend, then at a left-hand bend turn right onto path HB7 crossing a stile right of the gate into the St. George's Well car park. Now follow a left-hand fence to a gate and stile into Mill Wood. Go straight on through the wood, briefly joining the banks of the Evenlode by a spring. On reaching a footbridge, do NOT cross it but fork left onto a path following a right-hand ditch, soon passing a fenced plantation to your left and eventually bearing right and emerging from the wood by the corner of a fenced plantation. Here turn left onto path CM11 passing through a hedge gap then (on path HB7 again) following a grassy track along the outside edge of Mill Wood gradually climbing out of the valley, later with views to your right towards Combe. At the far end of the field follow the track bearing left into Abel Wood and climbing through it before levelling out to reach a track junction near the end of a village street in Long Hanborough called Millwood End.

Here turn right onto bridleway HB16 and follow this grassy track along the edge of Abel Wood towards East End for over a third of a mile, eventually ignoring a gate into the wood and entering a hedged lane which drops to the bottom of a dip. Now take bridleway NL11 straight on over a culvert then bear slightly left and follow a left-hand hedge uphill towards East End. On reaching a crossing powerline, turn right onto path NL9 rejoining **Walk A** and following the powerline across a field with fine views towards Combe ahead to reach the corner of a hedge. Now read the last paragraph.

Walk A follows this rough lane (bridleway HB14) straight on to two gates. Go through the bridlegate and turn right following the right-hand hedge. Some 40 yards short of the top right-hand corner of the field, turn right through a hedge gap then turn left and follow the left-hand hedge uphill to enter a green lane at Long Hanborough which later becomes a macadam road and leads you to the A4095. Turn left onto its pavement then, just after the left-hand houses end, cross the road and take path HB1 up the macadam drive to 'Elmwood'. Where the drive forks, turn left onto a path between a hedge and a low stone wall leading to a stile into a field with a view towards Wytham Hill ahead. Here bear half left across the field to a gate and stile in the far corner then bear slightly right across the next field joining a grassy track beside a right-hand hedge and following it to a corner of the field. Now turn right through a hedge gap and take a grassy track straight on past a barn. At the far side of the field go straight on through a hedge gap then turn right and follow a right-hand hedge to a corner of the field. Here turn left and follow the outside edge of Pinsley Wood to the next field corner where you turn left onto a grassy track which leads you to a gate and stile onto Lower Road.

Turn right onto this road. After some 90 yards turn right through a hedge gap onto path HB2 and bear half left passing between the third and fourth electricity poles in the field to reach a corner of Pinsley Wood. Bear slightly left along the outside edge of the wood to a slight outcrop then go straight on into a green lane (possibly concealed by nettles in summer). Where the lane enters the wood, fork right along a worn path for nearly 200 yards to a T-junction of paths near a stile to your left. Here turn left over the stile and follow a left-hand hedge with Church Hanborough coming into view ahead. On reaching the corner of a fence, follow it straight on, soon with a stone wall to your left, then continue along a drive to reach Church Road opposite the Norman church with its magnificent fourteenth-century tower and tall stone spire.

Turn right onto this road and after 150 yards, just past Mansell Close, turn left through a hedge gap onto narrow hedged path HB8. On emerging into a field, bear half right across it to the corner of a hedge then bear half left and follow a right-hand hedge downhill. At the bottom cross a concrete road, a culvert, a rail stile and a gravel track then go straight on uphill to a gap in the top hedge leading to Pigeon House Lane. Turn right onto this road and follow it for a quarter mile into Freeland. Opposite a stone cottage called 'Thrift Wood' turn right over a stile by a gate onto path FL5 following a right-hand hedge across a recreation ground to cross a stile leading to the end of Blenheim Lane. Turn left onto this road and take it to a T-junction with Wroslyn Road opposite the parish church dating from 1867.

Freeland, a corruption of 'Frithland' meaning 'woodland', is a village of relatively recent origin resulting from the enclosure of Eynsham Heath in 1781. This forced the scattered residents of the Heath, who in 1780 had rioted in protest at enclosure, to form a more concentrated settlement at Freeland which became the nucleus of the modern village. Quite small until 1945, Freeland has since expanded into an elongated straggling settlement which might easily become joined to its similar neighbour, Long Hanborough.

Turn right into Wroslyn Road then left into Broadmarsh Lane and go straight on until it turns right. Here continue on path FL7 towards woods known as Broad Marsh. By the back of the houses turn right beside the back garden fences for about 150 yards. 15 yards past the end of a macadam path to your right turn left onto a wide path into the woods and keep straight on for a third of a mile, passing a field to your left and later reaching a gate and stile into Cuckoo Lane. Turn right onto this road and follow it for two-thirds of a mile to the A4095. Cross this main road bearing slightly right and take concrete path NL14 virtually opposite straight on through the scrubland of North Leigh Common, otherwise called The Demesnes. After about 250 yards, on reaching a crossing path, turn right onto it, forking immediately left. Later, at a second fork, ignore a path to the left into a clearing then go straight on to reach a road at East End. Turn right onto this road and follow it for some 250 yards. Just before a postbox to your right, turn right through a hedge gap onto path NL9 bearing half left across a field to cross a ditch by an electricity pole. Now rejoining **Walk B** follow the powerline straight on to the corner of a hedge ahead.

Walks A and B now go through a hedge gap by an old stone stile and follow a right-hand hedge, later a left-hand fence straight on to enter a rough lane. Just before a triangular green turn right into another rough lane (path NL8). On entering a field, turn right and take a track downhill. At the bottom leave the track and go straight on into Abel Wood, soon crossing a footbridge and climbing to a T-junction. Here turn left onto path HB17 following a left-hand stream through the woods for nearly 300 yards. By a right-hand gate bear slightly left over a footbridge to join a track leading to a culvert, gate and stile. Cross these and take path NL13 bearing half left across a field to join the banks of the Evenlode at a bend. Now bear slightly right across the field to cross a stile and footbridge over the river left of a cottage.Take path CM4 over a further footbridge then, at a fork, bear right to reach a cottage drive. Turn left onto this and follow it for a third of a mile crossing a bridge over the railway and continuing to a bend in a road. Join this road and follow it straight on into Combe. On reaching the village green, fork left onto gravel path CM7 crossing the green to rejoin the road near the 'Cock Inn'.

WALK 28 :   WITNEY

Length of Walk: 5.8 miles / 9.3 Km
Starting Point: 'Windrush Inn', Witney
Grid Ref: SP347103
Maps: OS Landranger Sheet 164
OS Pathfinder Sheet 1091 (SP21/31)
How to get there / Parking: From the junction of the A4095 and
B4022 at Woodgreen north of Witney town centre, take the
A4095 (Bridge St./Mill St./Burford Rd.) towards Faringdon
for three-quarters of a mile and park in one of the left-hand
parking bays opposite the 'Windrush Inn'. Do not use the
pub car park without the landlord's permission.

Witney, on the banks of the River Windrush at the point where it
leaves the hills behind and enters the Thames Valley and where the
ancient London–Gloucester road crosses the Windrush before
climbing into the Cotswolds, has always formed a natural gateway
to the Cotswolds. As such it is hardly surprising that it should have
been here that a market developed for Cotswold wool and a
cloth-making industry became established as long as 1,000 years
ago. As a result, Witney prospered, as can be seen from its
magnificent thirteenth-century church with its tall spire, and by the
seventeenth century was renowned for its blanket-making. Despite
the industrialisation of the blanket-making industry with its
attendant mills and factories and the town's considerable expansion
and industrial diversification since 1945, Witney's centre with its
fine Cotswold-stone houses and civic buildings has remained a
place of character and interest which is well worth visiting before or
after your walk.

Starting on the edge of Witney, the walk explores the beautiful
section of the Windrush valley to the northwest of the town with
fine views in places throughout, following its southern slopes to the
fascinating riverside village of Minster Lovell with its ruined
mediaeval manor house and picturesque cottages. The return route
then takes you along the other side of the valley passing through
Crawley, which is attractive despite its old blanket mill, before

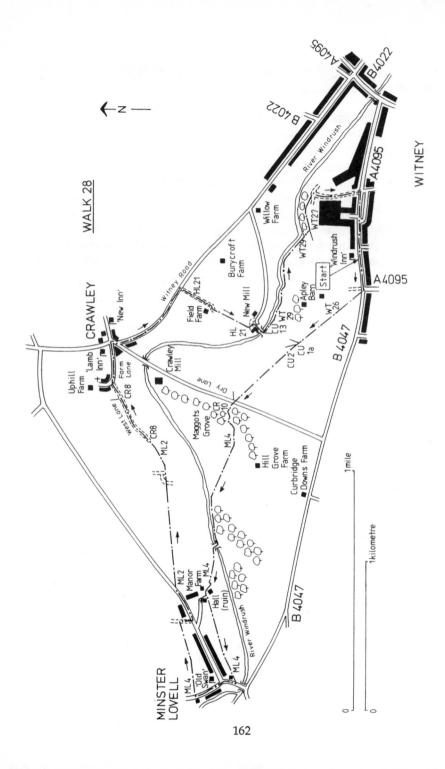

WALK 28

WITNEY

CRAWLEY

MINSTER LOVELL

New Mill
Willow Farm
Burycroft Farm
Field Farm
Crawley Mill
Uphill Farm
'Lamb Inn'
'New Inn'
Apley Barn
'Windrush Inn'
Start
Maggots Grove
Hill Grove Farm
Curbridge Downs Farm
Manor Farm
Hill (ruin)
'Old Swan'

Witney Road
Farm Lane
West Lane
Dry Lane
River Windrush

A 4095
B 4022
A 4095
B 4047
B 4047

HL 21
HL 21
ML 4
ML 2
ML 2
ML 4
ML 4
ML 4
ML 4
CR 8
CR 8
CR 10
CU 13
WT 29
CU 29
CU 1a
CU 2
WT 26
WT 27
WT 29

1 mile
1 kilometre

←—N—

162

crossing the Windrush at New Mill and following its banks back into Witney.

Starting from the 'Windrush Inn' on the edge of Witney, take the A4095 westwards with fine views across the Windrush valley to your right towards the distant spire of Leafield Church. At a mini-roundabout at its junction with the B4047 ignore a farm road to your right then fork immediately right onto bridleway WT26 following a left-hand hedge, later an earth bank downhill to cross a stile by a gate. Keep straight on along bridleway CU1a beside a left-hand hedge, then after some 60 yards fork left over a stile onto path CU2. Take this path straight on across the field over a rise where wide views of the Windrush valley open out with New Mill immediately to your right and Crawley with another old blanket mill in a hollow ahead, eventually reaching a gate into Dry Lane in a corner of the field.

Cross this road and a stile by a gate opposite onto path CR10 crossing a field to another stile. Here take path ML4 straight on into woodland, descending steeply to a gate and stile on the banks of a backwater of the Windrush. Now follow the banks of this stream straight on through three fields. On crossing a stile into the fourth field, leave the stream and follow a left-hand hedge straight on through two fields with the main River Windrush coming into view to your right. Now cross a stile by a gate into woodland and take an obvious path straight on. By a gate fork right descending to cross two footbridges and join the banks of the river. Continue through woodland close to the river to a bridge over it at a shallow weir where Minster Lovell Church and the ruined Hall come into view ahead. Cross the bridge and a stile and head for the ruins to cross a further footbridge and stile. Now bear left to a kissing-gate into the grounds of the ruined Hall.

Minster Lovell Hall and the nearby church are both thought to have been built by William Lord Lovell in the 1430s following the suppression of the nearby priory in 1415. This priory had been established by an earlier Lovell named Maud in the twelfth century and the priory together with this family are the source of the village's name. In 1487, following Francis Lovell's active support of Richard III at the Battle of Bosworth Field and later of the pretender Lambert Simnel at the Battle of Stoke, Minster Lovell Hall was confiscated by

Henry VII but legend has it that Francis, who disappeared after the Battle of Stoke, hid here in a locked secret room where he starved to death after the sudden death of his servant. This legend is supported by the discovery during restoration work in 1708 of a large underground vault in which a skeleton was found sitting at a table. Bought by the Coke family in 1602, the Hall was abandoned in the eighteenth century and used as farm buildings until it was acquired by the State in the 1930s to prevent further deterioration.

Now turn right and follow a right-hand fence, with a fifteenth-century stone dovecote and a barn with thirteenth-century buttresses to your right, to reach a corner of the ruins. Here take a paved path to the information office then turn left onto a fenced path into the churchyard. Still on path ML4, leave the main path and pass left of the church to cross a stone stile in the far wall of the churchyard. Now bear slightly left across a rough meadow to a stile in its far left-hand corner then turn right and follow a right-hand hedge to a gate and stile. Cross the stile then by the corner of a wall, bear slightly left to enter a recreation ground. Go straight across this to a gate onto a road left of the cricket pavilion. Turn right onto this road and follow it beside the Windrush into the picturesque village.

At a road junction by the 'Old Swan' bear slightly left passing a large converted farm building. Opposite a left-hand cottage turn right up a steep bank and over a concealed stile onto path ML1 following a right-hand hedge straight on through two fields. At the far end of the second field turn right onto a sunken grassy track and follow it beside a left-hand hedge to a road. Turn left onto this road and follow it for some 250 yards. After rounding a left-hand bend, look out for a concealed stile in the right-hand hedge. Turn right over this onto path ML2 bearing half left across a field to a stile then follow a left-hand stone wall straight on. At the far end of the field ignore a crossing track, go straight on over a stile and take a fenced path straight on over a hill, with Crawley coming into view ahead, to reach a rail stile. Here take path CR8 straight on beside a right-hand fence into a green lane called West Lane and follow it uphill for a third of a mile. On reaching a road called Farm Lane where there are fine views across Crawley village and the valley, turn right onto the road and follow it downhill to a crossroads near the 'Lamb Inn'.

Here turn right, then at a second junction fork left into Witney Road climbing out of the village. At the top of the hill round a left-hand bend then some 250 yards further on turn right onto the drive to Field Farm (path HL21). Take this track past farm buildings until it wiggles to the right and ends. Here go through the left-hand of two gates and take a fenced path downhill to cross a rail stile. Now follow a right-hand hedge straight on to a gate into the grounds of a cottage. Take the drive bearing left past the cottage then bear half right off the drive along a path beside the wall of New Mill to a handgate at the corner of the mill.

Here turn right onto a macadam drive beside the mill. Where its macadam surface ends, go straight on to a footbridge over the River Windrush. At the far end of this bridge turn left onto path CU13 along the riverbank to cross a footbridge and stile. Now take path WT29 following the riverbank through two more fields to a bend in the river where a pipeline crosses it. Here leave the riverbank and go straight on to reach the bottom of a steep bank then turn left onto path WT27 between the bottom of the bank and a line of willows to a gate. Go through this and take an enclosed path through scrubland to a junction of tracks then bear half right onto a gravel track which leads you uphill to the A4095 at Witney. Now turn right along this to your starting point.

WALK 29 :   LEAFIELD

Length of Walk: 12.0 miles / 19.3 Km
Starting Point: Road junction by Leafield Church.
Grid Ref: SP318153
Maps: OS Landranger Sheet 164
                   OS Pathfinder Sheet 1091 (SP21/31)
How to get there / Parking: Leafield, 4 miles northwest of
    Witney, may be reached from the town by taking the B4022
    towards Charlbury then forking left onto the Crawley road.
    In Crawley turn right then left passing the 'Lamb Inn' and
    following the priority road for over 3 miles to Leafield
    village green. Here find a suitable place to park in one of
    the side streets taking care not to obstruct the narrow roads
    or driveways or to park on grassy areas of the village green.

Leafield on the crest of the exposed ridge separating the Evenlode and Windrush valleys is best known for its radio masts and church spire which can be seen for miles around. Built by the renowned Victorian architect Sir George Gilbert Scott in 1860, Leafield is indeed one of his finest rural churches which takes full advantage of its hilltop location. The village with its cottages ranged around an attractive green with an ancient cross, like many of its neighbours such as Finstock and Ramsden, originated in the Middle Ages as a clearing in the royal forest of Wychwood, which in the thirteenth century still covered some eighty square miles of Oxfordshire from Woodstock to the Gloucestershire border. However it was not until after 1857 when the remaining ten square miles were 'disafforested' by an Act of Parliament and 2000 acres were felled and converted into farmland that the forest villages gained separate parish status and most of their churches were built.

The walk, which is the longest in the book but also one of the most attractive, explores the ancient Forest of Wychwood first taking you across a hill only cleared in 1857 into the Evenlode valley with its wide open views before climbing into what remains of Wychwood Forest and taking a beautiful path through the heart of it, won only after a 24-year battle principally fought by our

Society. You then continue through the forest villages of Finstock and Ramsden before returning to Leafield with superb views to the south across the Thames valley towards the Berkshire Downs.

Starting from the road junction by Leafield church at the eastern end of the village green, take Lower End eastwards for a quarter mile then turn left into Hatching Lane (signposted to Chadlington) and follow it downhill for half a mile into Fiveash Bottom. Having passed the start of the remaining part of Wychwood Forest to your right, turn left opposite a gate into bridleway CW3. This grassy stone former forest track initially follows the valley bottom then bears right and gradually climbs with views of Leafield on the ridge behind you. Ignore a branching track to your right and pass through Kingstanding Farm named after the wood it replaced.

At the top of the hill, where wide views begin to open out across a bend in the Evenlode valley towards Gloucestershire, the track (now AW18) becomes macadamed and continues downhill for two-thirds of a mile to a crossroads with the B4437. Turn right onto the B4437. After about 120 yards turn left through an old gateway onto bridleway AW14 and follow the left side of a fence downhill towards Ascott-under-Wychwood to a gate then keep straight on down the next field. About halfway down the field bear half left across it to a bridlegate near its bottom left-hand corner. Go through this and follow a right-hand fence straight on to a gap in a stone wall leading to London Lane on the edge of Ascott-under-Wychwood.

Ascott-under-Wychwood in the Evenlode valley is the one village on this walk which was outside the ancient forest and in consequence is the only one to have a Norman church. Indeed in the Middle Ages it must have been quite important as it can boast the sites of two mediaeval castles known as Ascott Earl and Ascott d'Oyley. Having a railway station on the Oxford–Worcester line opened in 1853, the village has expanded but retains some attractive old cottages.

Turn right onto this road. After 20 yards, just before the first right-hand bungalow, turn right again through a gap onto path AW12 following a fenced grass track and ignoring a branching track to your right. On reaching a hedge, turn left into a green lane called Mill Lane and follow it downhill to High Street. Turn right onto this road joining the southern route of the Oxfordshire Way. Where its surface changes to concrete at a left-hand bend, leave the road and bear slightly right across a field to its far corner. Here go through a hedge gap then turn sharp right and follow a right hand hedge to a corner of the field. Now turn left and follow the right-hand hedge around two further sides of the field. At the far end of the second side, go straight on through a hedge gap onto bridleway CL4 turning right then left and following a right-hand hedge towards Chilson to the far end of the field. Here go straight on through a hedge gap then turn left and follow a left-hand hedge around two sides of a field to reach the edge of Chilson where you take a walled lane straight on to the village street.

Leaving the Oxfordshire Way, turn right onto this road and take it straight on out of the village then uphill to the B4437. Turn right onto this road then, after some 70 yards, turn left onto a cul-de-sac road to Chilson Hill. Where the road ends by some cottages, take path CL3 straight on up a green lane. Having rounded a left-hand bend, turn immediately right through a hedge gap and follow a left-hand hedge. Where the hedge turns left, bear half left across a corner of the field to join a left-hand hedge and follow it uphill with fine views across the Evenlode valley behind you. At the top end of the field go straight on through a hedge gap and join a grassy track following it straight on uphill past a copse called Church Brake into the main area of Wychwood Forest at Knighton's Copse. On entering mature woodland, ignore branching tracks to left and right and continue up over the ridge until you reach a T-junction of tracks. Here turn left then immediately right onto a grassy track descending gently through a brackeny clearing known as Stag's Plain then continuing between a field hedge and the edge of the woodland. By a corner of the field at a junction of tracks, bear half left onto path CW2 still following the field hedge to reach a road at Sore Leap.

Turn left onto this road and follow it across a large forest clearing (in Wychwood known as a 'lawn') for nearly half a mile. Opposite the entrance to Waterman's Lodge Stables turn right over a stile by a gate onto path CW5 immediately forking right onto a track into mature woodland. After 150 yards at a second fork keep left then follow an obvious wide woodland track straight on for over three-quarters of a mile ignoring all crossing and branching tracks, with a field visible to your left at first and the track then widening into a grassy firebreak. On reaching a clearing by Vista Gate in the wall of Cornbury Park to your left, home in Elizabethan times to Robert Dudley, Earl of

Leicester, bear slightly right joining the gravel track from the gate. Follow this for a quarter mile ignoring all branching tracks and passing the Cornbury Estate Sawmills then descending to reach the end of a forest lake. Here turn left onto a stony track which climbs then ignore a branching track to the left. Near the top of the hill disregard a branching track to your right and a crossing track then take path FS4 straight on over a stile by Patch Hill Gate. Now ignore a branching track to your left, leave the woods behind and follow a grassy track known as Patch Riding for nearly half a mile, later with views of the Evenlode valley to your left, to reach the B4022 near Finstock church.

Finstock, first recorded in 1135 as being one of the Wychwood villages created through 'assarting' or making enclosed clearings in the forest, though somewhat spoilt by poor modern development, has a fine seventeenth-century gabled stone manor house and a church built in 1842 as a chapel-of-ease to Charlbury parish before the 'disafforestation'.

Cross the B4022 and take path FS11, a green lane opposite, straight on past the church into a scrubby field where you continue ahead along a worn path beside a left-hand hedge. On nearing a housing estate, follow the path turning left then beside a left-hand fence past an adventure playground and the village school to reach School Road. Turn right onto this and keep straight on down Well Hill. At the bottom of the hill at a road junction turn left onto the road signposted to Wilcote and North Leigh. At a second junction by the 'Plough Inn' take path FS13 straight on up a gravel drive towards the pub car park. Just past the pub, where the drive turns left, leave it and go straight on up a grassy bank soon wiggling to your right to cross a rail stile into a field. Now follow a right-hand stone wall to cross some more rails then turn right onto a grassy track beside a right-hand hedge. Where both turn right, turn left across the field to a gap at a bend in the far hedge. Take path RM2 straight on through this gap and across the next field to an ash tree where you turn left to reach the corner of a hedge. Follow this hedge straight on to a field corner where you continue past the end of a barbed-wire fence then turn right and follow the fence to cross a wooden fence. Now bear half left across a paddock to pass through a concealed gate in the far left-hand corner left of a long stone building. Here take a gravel drive straight on to white gates leading to Wilcote Lane in Ramsden, part of Akeman

Street, a Roman road from London via Bicester to Cirencester.

Turn right onto this road and follow it for some 250 yards to a crossroads by the 'Royal Oak'. Here cross the major road and take the road opposite (still part of Akeman Street) straight on past the church, built by A W Blomfield in 1872, for nearly a mile, later with wide views to your left towards North Leigh, Witney and the Berkshire Downs beyond. At a junction with the B4022 near Whiteoak Green cross the major road and, leaving Akeman Street, take a concrete road between buildings at New Found Out Farm opposite to enter a narrow green lane (CR2). Follow this lane called Pay Lane straight on for over a mile passing Blindwell Wood to your left to reach the end of Greenwich Lane by Greenwich Farm.

Turn right onto this road then immediately left onto concealed path LD8 leading between a cottage and a stone wall into a field. By the far end of the cottage bear slightly left onto a grassy strip separating two fields with wide views towards the Berkshire Downs opening out to your left, later bearing half right by the end of a hedge and eventually reaching a stile. Cross this and follow the right-hand edge of the next field past some farm buildings to cross a stile by a gate then go through another gate by a thatched cottage into Witney Lane. Turn right onto this road then, on rounding a right-hand bend, turn left over a concealed stile onto path LD7 and follow a right-hand hedge with fine views to your left towards the Berkshire Downs. On reaching a stile in a stone wall, cross it and turn left onto path LD5. Having crossed another stile by a gate, bear slightly right to cross a further stile by a gate then follow a right hand hedge. At the far end of the field cross a stile and turn right onto worn path LD1 crossing a corner of the field to a pair of wooden posts then continuing through scrub to a stile into an enclosed path leading to Leafield Green. Here turn right for your starting point.

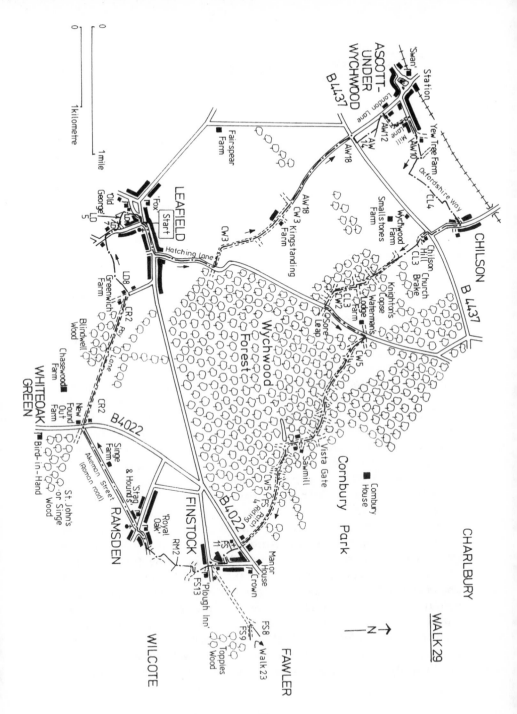

171

WALK 30 : BURFORD

Length of Walk: (A) 9.0 miles / 14.5 Km
(B) 5.7 miles / 9.2 Km

Starting Point: Entrance to public car park at junction of Church Lane and Guildenford, Burford.

Grid Ref: SP253123

Maps: OS Landranger Sheet 163
OS Pathfinder Sheet 1091 (SP21/31)

How to get there / Parking: From the roundabout at the junction of the A40 and A361, take the A361 into Burford. Just past the 'Cotswold Arms' turn right into Church Lane and follow it to a signposted free car park.

Burford, spreading up the southern slopes of the Windrush valley from its river bridge, has, with some justification, been described as one of the most beautiful towns in the Cotswolds and the reasons for this are to be found in its history. Only a village at the time of the Domesday Book, Burford had by 1100 become a market town. This soon led the town to become prosperous as a centre for the wool trade and saddle-making and this wealth can be seen both in the numerous fine stone houses built by the merchants and the church which, though Norman in origin, was lavishly refurbished and given its tall spire in the fifteenth century. Added variety is given to the town by a number of half-timbered buildings using the plentiful supply of oak from nearby Wychwood Forest. Until the 1850s when 'disafforestation' led to the clearance of much of the ancient royal forest, Wychwood had extended to within a mile of the town and legend has it that poachers from Burford frequently stole venison from the forest and hid it in stone tombs in the churchyard to evade capture. In 1649 the church became the scene of one of the last acts of the Civil War when a group of 400 'Levellers', who had mutinied against Cromwell in protest at his authoritarian tendencies, were captured and held in the church and three of their number were executed. In 1812 Burford, which in the eighteenth century had profited from numerous stagecoaches frequenting its inns, was bypassed by a new turnpike road avoiding the steep hills on either side of the town and later the railways also passed it by, so that the town was spared the expansion and industrialisation characteristic of the nineteenth century and has preserved the olde-worlde charm so appreciated by modern tourists.

Both walks take you across the Windrush to Fulbrook before exploring the south-western corner of what was once Wychwood Forest and dropping down to the deserted village of Widford in the Windrush valley. Walk A then takes you along a beautiful quiet section of the valley to explore the picturesque villages of Swinbrook and Asthall before climbing its southern slopes to reach Stonelands and dropping down again into the valley at Widford. Both walks then return through pleasant riverside meadows into Burford.

Both walks start from the entrance to the car park and fork right into Church Lane following it round a right-hand bend to Church Green. Here go straight on to the churchyard gates then turn left into an alleyway round the edge of the churchyard into Lawrence Lane. Now turn left to reach the High Street (A361). Turn right onto this crossing Burford Bridge over the Windrush where you should stop in the alcove on the bridge to look at the beautiful river scene. At a roundabout fork right and take the A361 uphill into Fulbrook with views across Burford to your right. Having passed Meadow End, go past a cottage then turn right onto path FU6 crossing two stiles then bearing left across a long paddock to a kissing-gate in the far corner. Now follow a fenced path with views across the Windrush valley to your right to cross a stone stile then follow a left-hand fence and wall passing iron gates to reach a stone stile in the wall. Turn left over this onto path FU5 and follow a right-hand wall to a corner of the field. Here turn right over a stone stile onto a drive and follow it to Meadow Lane. Turn left onto this passing left of Fulbrook war memorial to the A361.

Cross the main road and take Church Lane straight on to a kissing-gate into the churchyard. Go through this and take grassy path FU1 bearing slightly left past the twelfth-century church with a later tower to cross a stone stile in the back wall of the churchyard. Now bear half right across a meadow to a gate and stile then keep straight on to a gate and stone stile leading to Upper End. Turn right onto this road then left onto the A361. At the far end of a high stone

173

wall to your right, turn right over a low stone wall onto path FU7 bearing half left across wasteland to the corner of a field then turn right and join a right-hand hedge. After some 250 yards, where the hedge bears slightly right, leave it bearing slightly left along a dip between the hills, gradually bearing left to reach the far left-hand corner of the field. Go straight on through the left-hand of two hedge gaps then bear half right across the next field to a corner. Here go through a hedge gap and take path SW10 bearing half left across a field with superb views to your right towards the Berkshire Downs and Didcot Power Station some 20 miles away, passing right of an electricity junction pole to reach a gate into Widley Copse, part of the ancient royal forest of Wychwood.

Turn right here onto path SW5 and take this stony track through Widley Copse. On leaving the wood, where there is another fine view towards the Berkshire Downs to your right, take a winding stony, later macadamed lane straight on for over half a mile ignoring all branching tracks and passing a row of cottages and Pains Farm. At a sharp left-hand bend turn right into a walled stony lane (SW6) and follow it uphill to a gate into a field called Handley Plain. Here take a stony track straight on over the hill past a wood called Faw's Grove with wide views to the south towards Swinbrook, the A40 and the Berkshire Downs before descending to gates in the bottom of a dip. Now take a green lane straight on uphill to reach a road. Turn right onto this road. After some 300 yards, soon after woodland begins to your left, turn left over a stone stile by a gate onto path SW4. Now follow a grassy track between woods down Dean Bottom to a gate and ladder-stile, then continue past Widford Church to a crossing grassy track (path SW1) near the right-hand corner of a cottage garden, onto which **Walk A** turns left and **Walk B** turns right.

Widford, until 1844 a detached parish of Gloucestershire, can today be considered as a deserted village, as apart from the church there are only two farms and a few scattered cottages, but foundations of the mediaeval village can be discerned in the field west of the church and in nearby woodland. The twelfth-century church, which became disused in 1859 but was restored in 1904, can boast some fourteenth-century wall paintings and fragments of a Roman mosaic pavement in its floor suggesting that it was built on the site of a Roman villa. This belief has also been strengthened by Roman objects being found by gravediggers.

Walk B follows this track past the church, the site of the lost village and a lake to reach a road, then turns left onto it crossing a bridge over the Windrush to reach a T-junction where it turns right to rejoin Walk A. Now read the last paragraph.

Walk A follows the track into and through a second field to a gate and stile. In the third field, having crossed a tiny stream, fork right onto a grassy path to a small gate in a stone wall ahead. Now follow a walled path straight on between the grounds of Swinbrook vicarage and the site of a mansion built by the Fettiplace family in about 1490 but which disappeared after the family died out in 1805. By a cottage turn left passing left of the cottage and going through a white gate into the churchyard. Now turn right along a stony path past the grave of the twentieth-century authoress Nancy Mitford and the twelfth-century church, which was altered over the following centuries and contains various monuments to the Fettiplace family, to reach Swinbrook village street.

Turn right onto this and follow its winding course passing a stone building with a weather vane depicting a witch on a broomstick and a lake once used for breeding freshwater mussels. Ignore a turning to your left and continue along the road to the 'Swan'. Here turn left over a stone stile opposite the pub onto path SW3 and bear half right across a field to cross two stiles left of a hedge at the far end of the field, then follow a left-hand wall and fence. Where these turn left, leave them and go straight on across the field to a stile left of two tall poplars. Here take path AS4 bearing slightly right across the next field, heading left of a line of willow trees with views to your right in places of Asthall Manor with its mullioned windows, built in 1620 and from 1919 home of Lord Redesdale, the father of Nancy Mitford, and the twelfth-century parish church with its fifteenth-century tower which contains a mediaeval stone altar and a fourteenth-century effigy of Lady Jane Cornwall, whose family then owned the village. By the willow trees pass a bend in the River Windrush then bear slightly right to a stone stile onto a road left of the river bridge. Turn right onto this road crossing the bridge, ignoring a turning to the left and entering Asthall village.

At a fork by a small green and the sixteenth-century 'Maytime Inn' bear left and continue to a T-junction. Here leave the road and take path AS2, a stony track, which follows the approximate course of Akeman Street, the Roman road from London via Bicester to Cirencester, straight on past farm buildings and through two fields. At the far end of the second field follow the track bearing right into a third field then leave the track and take path SW8 beside a left-hand wall then a copse, bearing left to a corner of the field. Here go straight on through a hedge gap and follow the left-hand fence and wall uphill to a hedge gap leading to the A40 at a turning for Brize Norton. Cross the A40 and a stone stile on the right-hand side of the entrance to the Brize Norton road then, ignoring a wide hedge gap to your right, go straight on through a somewhat overgrown hedge gap and take path AS2 (later BN10) following a right-hand hedge straight on towards Stonelands with views towards the Berkshire Downs opening out ahead.

Some 100 yards short of the far end of the field turn right over a stone stile onto path SN2 and bear slightly right across a field to a gap in the hedge ahead. Here cross a wooden fence and go straight on across two paddocks, crossing a series of wooden fences to reach a gap in a line of trees ahead. Now keep straight on to the far corner of the next paddock where you cross a further wooden fence, turn right onto bridleway BF16 and take this stony track past a quarry to the A40. Cross this and take bridleway SW2 straight on through a gate and along a grassy track through four fields with views towards distant Wytham Hill to your right in the first and later to your left up the Windrush valley towards Burford and across the valley towards Widford, Swinbrook, Wychwood Forest and the distant spire of Leafield Church ahead and to your right. Having passed through gates into Widford Mill Farm, bear slightly right in the farmyard to join a macadam drive and follow it to a road junction at Widford where you turn left rejoining **Walk B**.

Walks A and B follow this road to a slight left-hand bend then leave it taking path SW9 straight on over a stile by a gate and following the banks of the Windrush to a stile and footbridge. Now take worn path BF17 straight on for two-thirds of a mile, generally following the banks of the Windrush but cutting off some of its bends until you cross a second footbridge. Here bear slightly left across a meadow to a stile onto a road which before 1812 was the main London–Gloucester turnpike. Turn right onto it and follow it for over half a mile into Burford to reach the 'Royal Oak'. Here turn right into a street called Guildenford and follow it to reach the car park.

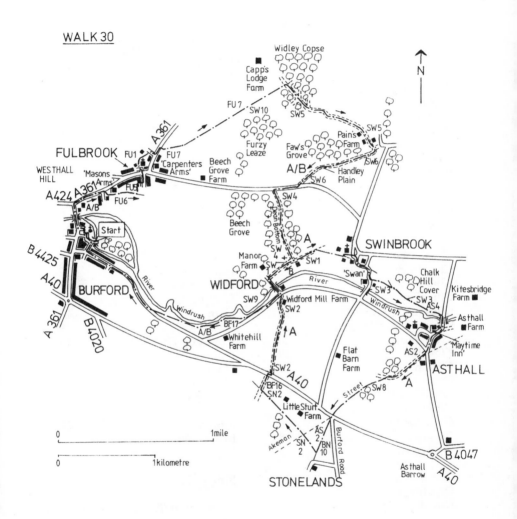

WALK 30

INDEX OF PLACE NAMES

The Book Castle publishes a wide range of walks books for OXFORDSHIRE, BEDFORDSHIRE, BUCKINGHAMSHIRE and HERTFORDSHIRE. See the list of publications at the end of this book.

*

The following pages feature a selection of the various index maps.

Index Map for OXFORDSHIRE WALKS book two:
OXFORD, THE DOWNS and
THE THAMES VALLEY

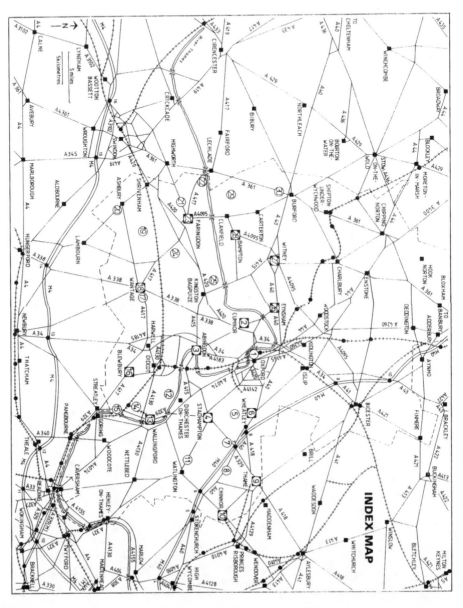

Index Map for CHILTERN WALKS book one:
HERTFORDSHIRE, BEDFORDSHIRE and
NORTH BUCKINGHAMSHIRE

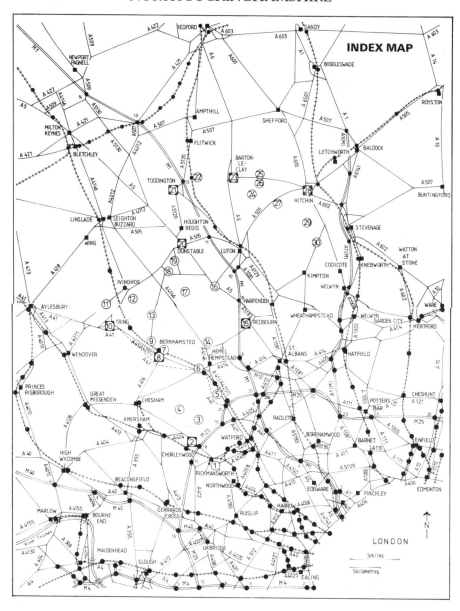

Index Map for CHILTERN WALKS book two:
BUCKINGHAMSHIRE

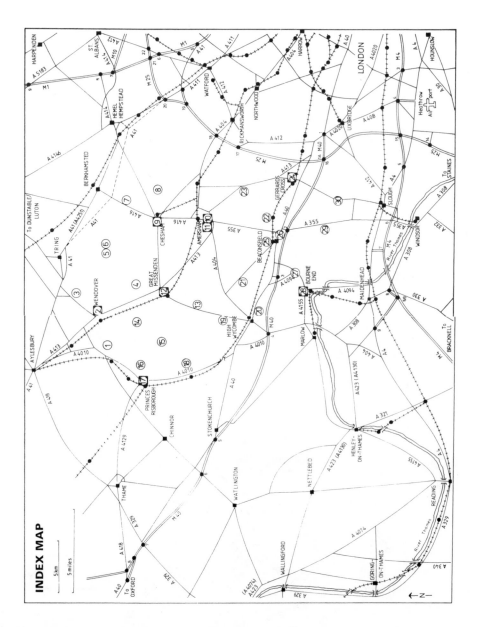

Index Map for CHILTERN WALKS book three:
OXFORDSHIRE and WEST BUCKINGHAMSHIRE

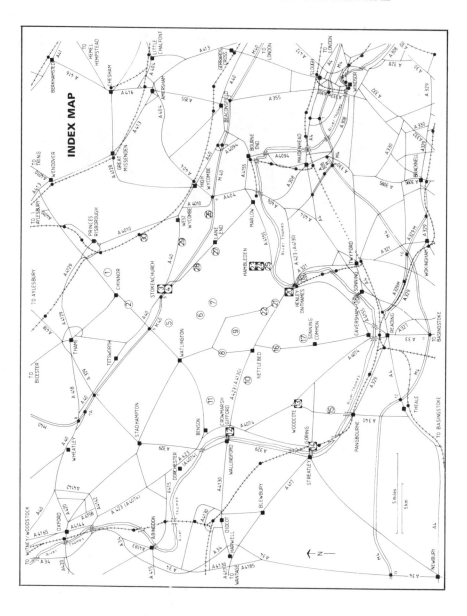

Index Map for FAMILY WALKS book one:
CHILTERNS SOUTH

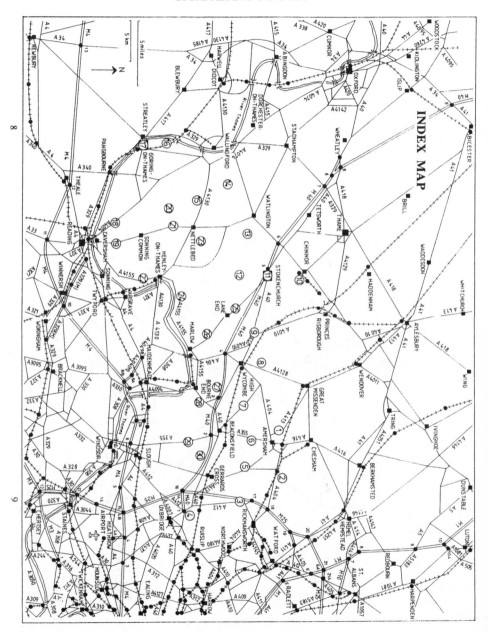

Index Map for LOCAL WALKS book one:
SOUTH BEDFORDSHIRE and NORTH CHILTERNS

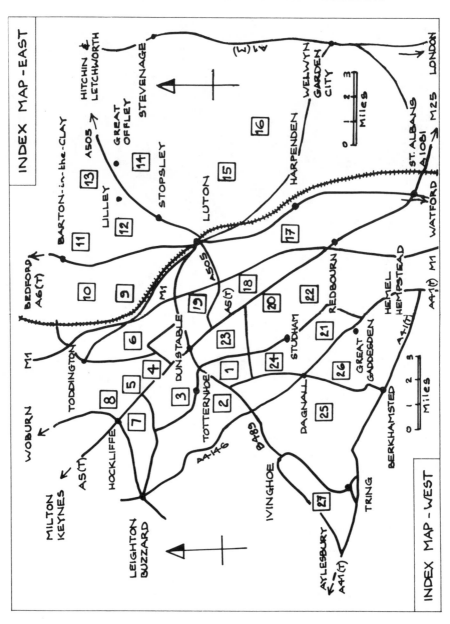

Index Map for LOCAL WALKS book two:
NORTH and MID-BEDFORDSHIRE

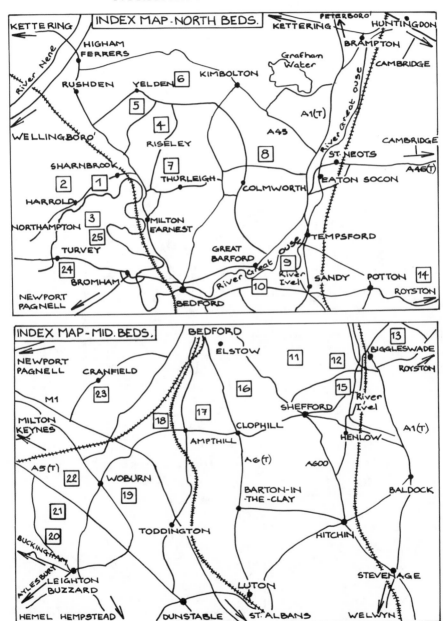

Index Map for PUB WALKS from Country Stations:
BUCKINGHAMSHIRE and OXFORDSHIRE

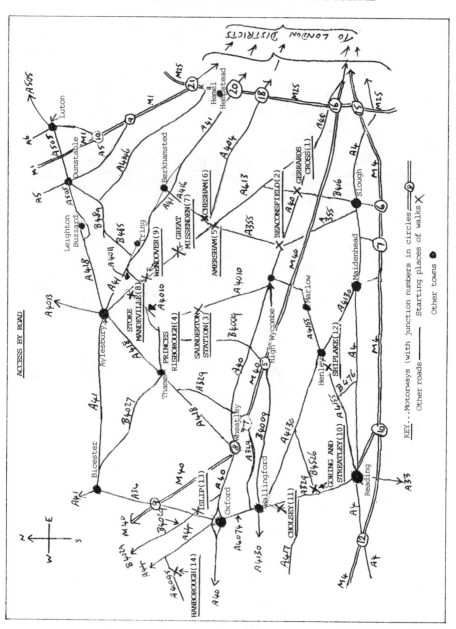

Books Published by
THE BOOK CASTLE

COUNTRYSIDE CYCLING IN BEDFORDSHIRE,
BUCKINGHAMSHIRE AND HERTFORDSHIRE: Mick Payne.
Twenty rides on- and off-road for all the family.

PUB WALKS FROM COUNTRY STATIONS:
Bedfordshire and Hertfordshire: Clive Higgs.
Fourteen circular country rambles, each starting and finishing at a
railway station and incorporating a pub-stop at a mid-way point.

PUB WALKS FROM COUNTRY STATIONS:
Buckinghamshire and Oxfordshire: Clive Higgs.
A further selection of unusual rural rambles.

LOCAL WALKS: South Bedfordshire and North Chilterns:
Vaughan Basham.
Twenty-seven thematic circular walks.

LOCAL WALKS: North and Mid Bedfordshire: Vaughan Basham.
Twenty-five thematic circular walks.

FAMILY WALKS: Chilterns South: Nick Moon.
Thirty 3 to 5 mile circular walks.

FAMILY WALKS: Chilterns North: Nick Moon.
Thirty further shortish country walks.

CHILTERN WALKS: Hertfordshire, Bedfordshire and
North Buckinghamshire: Nick Moon.
CHILTERN WALKS: Buckinghamshire: Nick Moon.
CHILTERN WALKS: Oxfordshire and West Buckinghamshire:
Nick Moon.
A trilogy of circular walks, in association with the Chiltern Society.
Each volume contains 30 circular walks.

OXFORDSHIRE WALKS:
Oxford, the Cotswolds and the Cherwell Valley: Nick Moon.
OXFORDSHIRE WALKS:
Oxford, the Downs and the Thames Valley: Nick Moon.
Two volumes that complement Chiltern Walks: Oxfordshire and
complete coverage of the county, in association with the Oxford
Fieldpaths Society. Thirty circular walks in each.

JOURNEYS INTO BEDFORDSHIRE: Anthony Mackay.
Foreword by The Marquess of Tavistock, Woburn Abbey. A lavish book of over 150 evocative ink drawings.

MANORS and MAYHEM, PAUPERS and PARSONS: Tales from Four Shire: Beds., Bucks., Herts., and Northants.: John Houghton
Little-known historical snippets and stories.

MYTHS and WITCHES, PEOPLE and POLITICS: Tales from Four Shires: Bucks., Beds., Herts., and Northants.: John Houghton.
Anthology of strange, but true historical events.

HISTORIC FIGURES IN THE BUCKINGHAMSHIRE LANDSCAPE: John Houghton.
Major personalities and events that have shaped the county's past, including a special section on Bletchley Park.

FOLK: Characters and Events in the History of Bedfordshire and Northamptonshire: Vivienne Evans.
Anthology about people of yesteryear – arranged alphabetically by village or town.

BEDFORDSHIRE'S YESTERYEARS Vol 2:
The Rural Scene: Brenda Fraser Newstead.
Vivid first-hand accounts of country life two or three generations ago.

BEDFORDSHIRE'S YESTERYEARS Vol 3:
Craftsmen and Tradespeople: Brenda Fraser Newstead.
Fascinating recollections over several generations practising many vanishing crafts and trades.

BEDFORDSHIRE'S YESTERYEARS Vol 4:
Wat Times and Civil Matters: Brenda Fraser Newstead.
Two World Wars, plus transport, law and order, etc.

THE RAILWAY AGE IN BEDFORDSHIRE: Fred Cockman.
Classic, illustrated account of early railway history.

GLEANINGS REVISITED:
Nostalgic Thoughts of a Bedfordshire Farmer's Boy:
E W O'Dell.
His own sketches and early photographs adorn this lively account of rural Bedfordshire in days gone by.

FARM OF MY CHILDHOOD, 1925–1947: Mary Roberts.
An almost vanished lifestyle on a remote farm near Flitwick.

SWANS IN MY KITCHEN: Lis Dorer.
Story of a Swan Sanctuary near Hemel Hempstead.

DUNSTABLE WITH THE PRIORY: 1100–1550: Vivienne Evans.
Dramatic growth of Henry I's important new town around a major crossroads.

DUNSTABLE DECADE: THE EIGHTIES:
A Collection of Photographs: Pat Lovering.
A souvenir book of 300 pictures of people and events in the 1980s.

DUNSTABLE IN DETAIL: Nigel Benson.
A hundred of the town's buildings and features, plus town trail map.

OLD DUNSTABLE: Bill Twaddle.
A new edition of this collection of early photographs.

BOURNE and BRED: A Dunstable Boyhood Between the Wars:
Colin Bourne.
An elegantly written, well-illustrated book capturing the spirit of the town over fifty years ago.

ROYAL HOUGHTON: Pat Lovering:
Illustrated history of Houghton Regis from the earliest times to the present.

THE CHANGING FACE OF LUTON: An Illustrated History:
Stephen Bunker, Robin Holgate and Marian Nichols.
Luton's development from earliest times to the present busy industrial town. Illustrated in colour and monochrome

THE MEN WHO WORE STRAW HELMETS:
Policing Luton, 1840–1974: Tom Madigan.
Meticulously chronicled history; dozens of rare photographs; author served in Luton Police for fifty years.

BETWEEN THE HILLS: The Story of Lilley, a Chiltern Village:
Roy Pinnock.
A priceless piece of our heritage – the rural beauty remains but the customs and way of life described here have largely disappeared.

A HATTER GOES MAD!: Kristina Howells.
Luton Town footballers, officials and supporters talk to a female fan.

LEGACIES: Tales and Legends of Luton and the North Chilterns:
Vic Lea.
Twenty-five mysteries and stories based on fact, including Luton Town Football Club. Many photographs.

LEAFING THROUGH LITERATURE:
Writers' Lives in Hertfordshire and Bedfordshire: David Carroll.
Illustrated short biographies of many famous authors and their connections with these counties.

A PILGRIMAGE IN HERTFORDSHIRE: H M Alderman.
Classic, between-the-wars tour round the county, embellished with line drawings.

CHILTERN ARCHAEOLOGY: RECENT WORK:
A Handbook for the Next Decade: edited by Robin Holgate.
The latest views, results and excavations by twenty-three leading archaeologists throughout the Chilterns.

THE HILL OF THE MARTYR:
An Architectural History of St. Albans Abbey: Eileen Roberts.
Scholarly and readable chronological narrative history of Hertfordshire and Bedfordshire's famous cathedral. Fully illustrated with photographs and plans.

THE TALL HITCHIN SERGEANT:
A Victorian Crime Novel Based on Fact: Edgar Newman.
Mixes real police officers and authentic background with an exciting storyline.

THE TALL HITCHIN INSPECTOR'S CASEBOOK:
A Victorian Crime Novel Based on Fact: Edgar Newman.
Worthies of the time encounter more archetypal villains.

SPECIALLY FOR CHILDREN

VILLA BELOW THE KNOLLS: A Story of Roman Britain:
Michael Dundrow.
An exciting adventure for young John in Totternhoe and Dunstable two thousand years ago.

THE RAVENS: One Boy Against the Might of Rome:
James Dyer.
On the Barton Hills and in the south-east of England as the men of the great fort of Ravensburgh (near Hexton) confront the invaders.

Further titles are in preparation.
All the above are available via any bookshop, or from the publisher and bookseller

THE BOOK CASTLE
12 Church Street, Dunstable Bedfordshire, LU5 4RU
Tel: (01582) 605670